PUZZLE BOXES

FUN AND INTRIGUING BAND SAW PROJECTS

JEFF VOLLMER

POPULAR WOODWORKING BOOKS
CINCINNATI, OHIO
www.popularwoodworking.com

READ THIS IMPORTANT SAFETY NOTICE

To prevent accidents, keep safety in mind while you work. Use the safety guards installed on power equipment; they are for your protection.

When working on power equipment, keep fingers away from saw blades, wear safety goggles to prevent injuries from flying wood chips and sawdust, wear hearing protection and consider installing a dust vacuum to reduce the amount of airborne sawdust in your woodshop.

Don't wear loose clothing, such as neckties or shirts with loose sleeves, or jewelry, such as rings, necklaces or bracelets, when working on power equipment. Tie back long hair to prevent it from getting caught in your equipment.

People who are sensitive to certain chemicals should check the chemical content of any product before using it.

Due to the variability of local conditions, construction materials, skill levels, etc., neither the author nor Popular Woodworking Books assumes any responsibility for any accidents, injuries, damages or other losses incurred resulting from the material presented in this book.

The authors and editors who compiled this book have tried to make the contents as accurate and correct as possible. Plans, illustrations, photographs and text have been carefully checked. All instructions, plans and projects should be carefully read, studied and understood before beginning construction.

Prices listed for supplies and equipment were current at the time of publication and are subject to change.

METRIC CONVERSION CHART

TO CONVERT	TO	MULTIPLY BY
Inches	Centimeters	2.54
Centimeters	Inches	0.4
Feet	Centimeters	30.5
Centimeters	Feet	0.03
Yards	Meters	0.9
Meters	Yards	1.1

Distributed in Canada by Fraser Direct
100 Armstrong Avenue
Georgetown, Ontario L7G 5S4
Canada

Distributed in the U.K. and Europe by David & Charles
Brunel House
Newton Abbot
Devon TQ12 4PU
England
Tel: (+44) 1626 323200
Fax: (+44) 1626 323319
E-mail: postmaster@davidandcharles.co.uk

Distributed in Australia by Capricorn Link
P.O. Box 704
Windsor, NSW 2756
Australia

Visit our website at www.popularwoodworking.com or our consumer website at www.fwbookstore.com for more woodworking information and other arts and crafts projects.

Other fine Popular Woodworking Books are available from your local bookstore or direct from the publisher.

14   13   12   11   10   5   4   3   2   1

Library of Congress Cataloging-in-Publication Data

Vollmer, Jeff.
  Puzzle boxes : 12 fun and intriguing band saw projects / by Jeff Vollmer. -- 1st ed.
        p. cm.
  ISBN 978-1-55870-847-1 (hardcover : alk. paper)
1. Woodwork. 2. Wooden boxes. 3. Band saws. I. Title.
TT200.V65 2009
684'.08--dc22

                                2009032577

ACQUISITIONS EDITOR: David Thiel, david.thiel@gmail.com
SENIOR EDITOR: Jim Stack, jim.stack@gmail.com
DESIGNER: Brian Roeth
PRODUCTION COORDINATOR: Mark Griffin
PHOTOGRAPHERS: Lynn and Alexandra Vollmer
PROJECT OPENER PHOTOS: Al Parrish

ABOUT THE AUTHORS

Jeff Vollmer was born and raised in Cincinnati, Ohio, and attended the University of Cincinnati College Conservatory of Music. He made his first puzzle box in 1989. This was the beginning of Royal Woods, his own part-time business. In 1992 he made a full-time commitment to making band-sawn boxes and Royal Woods really took off. Today, Jeff and his wife, Lynn, work together making puzzle boxes and selling them at art shows and in fine galleries. Their work is represented in all 50 states and in Europe. Jeff has written articles for *Popular Woodworking* magazine, teaches classes in his shop and at Mark Adams School of Woodworking in Franklin, Indiana.

DEDICATION

The book is dedicated to the two men who inspired in me the love of wood and woodworking. The first is Ken Hermann, a neighbor and family friend who was always around when I was growing up. He was a master carpenter and showed me how to use tools and how to do a job "right". He is gone now, but a few of his tools remain in my possession. I think of him often as I work. The second man is Ed Keller, my wife's cousin. Ed, too, is gone, but he taught me much. He was lovably eccentric and a perfectionist to the end. From him, I got my knowledge of making glue seams disappear. Nothing can be sanded too well!

I miss the men, but their memories live on just a little in every box I create.

ACKNOWLEDGEMENTS

This book was a learning experience for my whole family. We all take part in the box-making business, so we all took part in the making of this book. My wife Lynn orchestrated the video and photography. Our daughter Alexandra transcribed the text and took lots of photos. Out youngest daughter, Sydney, let us use her video camera and showed Lynn how to use the software.

A Few Terms

Burl - The part of a tree that is 6" above ground and below.

Blank - Any solid piece of wood that has been prepared to be cut into a box.

Deft™ Step Saver - A second-generation Danish oil. With approximately 60% more solids than conventional Danish oil, it makes the best pre-finish for any box.

Divider Key - A small inner divider with a dowel coming out the bottom. When lifted, this piece releases a spring-loaded drawer.

DonJer Suede Tex (flocking) - Ground felt fibers that get sprayed into a box to form a felt lining.

Flapper Sander - Like a bench grinder but it has large, 4"-wide sanding heads that use a serrated sandpaper backed with brushes. This tool is used to sand irregular and/or hard-to-get-to places without changing the contour of the wood.

The Front of the Box - The end where the first key is removed.

Guts - The chunk of wood cut out from the middle of a box to form the cavity or chamber.

Joiner - Small piece of wood reglued into the box to join the box back together at the point where the saw cut in to hollow it out.

The Key - Any puzzle piece that lifts vertically to unlock each box or sliding piece.

Shoulders - Thin pieces of wood cut from the guts and reglued to the inside of a box to hold up the inner lid.

Tear out - This is the result of a band saw blade exiting the wood.

TABLE OF CONTENTS

SECTION ONE

10 The Band Saw

13 The Wood

14 Using Magnets to Conceal

16 Preparing Box Blanks

17 Band-Saw Practice

24 Making Our First Box

38 The Next Step Up

SECTION TWO

49   The King's Safe

68   Box in a Log

82   Round-Drawer Spring Box

96   Two-Drawer Spring Safe

118   Holes are Cool

126   Ultimate Jewelry Box

142   *Suppliers*

143   *Index*

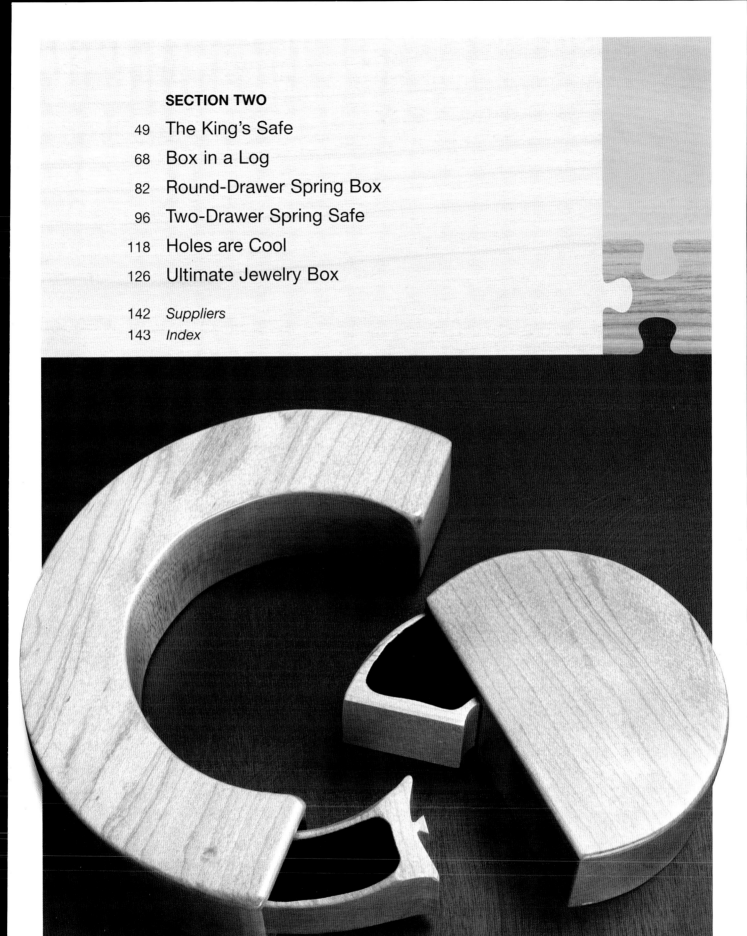

INTRODUCTION

IT WAS BY HAPPY CIRCUMSTANCE THAT MY WIFE, LYNN, AND I STARTED creating our fun and unique puzzle (and puzzling) boxes. We had both been hobbyist artists while working "real" jobs at the same company. On a lark, we and a group of friends decided to take our wares to the first Ohio Renaissance Festival back in 1990. We built a medieval shop. Our friends were selling juggling sticks and stained glass, I had wood turnings and Lynn had crafted wooden jewelry made from unused pieces from the turnings.

The first week my turnings were a huge success. I was sure I had found my new true calling. The next week I wasn't so sure — nothing sold. In a fit of frustration, I went to the basement (my shop at that point) and hurriedly cut a piece of wood into a box. It was based on one that my wife had admired on our honeymoon many years before, but mine was far more elaborate. (I am German — if a little bit is good then a lot must be better, so I added more details to the original concept.) I came upstairs with the box, handed it to my wife (she says I slammed it on the counter) and asked her if she thought it would sell. She thought it was a great idea, so we made a few to sell the following weekend. I made a few the next night and we glued them up the next evening. We stained them and were still spraying lacquer on them in the van on the way to the show! They sold within minutes of our booth opening.

We made more boxes that night and they sold again within the first few minutes of opening at the show. My turnings were still not selling, so we decided to spend the next week making as many boxes as possible. Again, they all sold — we knew we had a hit.

I gave up the woodturning business and hit the art-show circuit with our boxes. As fate would have it, within a year of making and selling the first boxes, my wife and I both lost our jobs due to our company's downsizing. We decided to devote our time and energies to making these fun and beautiful boxes.

As time passed I started to become more and more creative. Our boxes have gone from a simple lock-and-slide style to complex puzzles, some featuring hidden drawers, some with spring-loaded drawers, some with drawers that use magnets and the ones people consider most creative — the round-drawer boxes.

Spend some of your free time with us as we show you how to make some puzzle boxes of your own. None of this is rocket science. It requires a few tools, an open mind and a pair of willing hands. Have fun!

SECTION ONE

10 **The Band Saw**

13 **The Wood**

14 **Using Magnets to Conceal**

16 **Preparing Box Blanks**

17 **Band-Saw Practice**

24 **Making Our First Box**

38 **The Next Step Up**

For making puzzle boxes, the best band saw to use is a 14" two-wheel saw. I prefer the 14" Delta. Smaller band saws are not good because they have a shorter blade which causes it to heat up faster, thus shortening blade life. And, the motor is too small to cut thick wood. Larger band saws are not good because you cannot buy an ⅛" blade without special ordering. Also, the thinner blades do not track well on a saw larger than 14".

The Band Saw

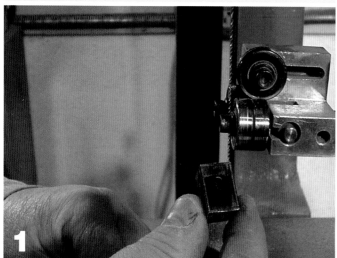

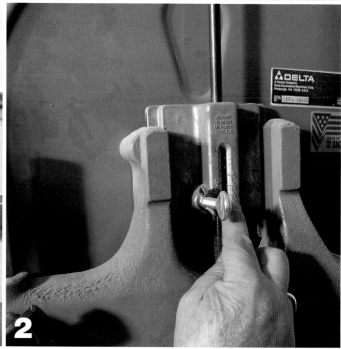

STEP 1   When you bought your saw, it probably had metal blocks for blade guides. These should be replaced with synthetic, non-metallic blocks, that reduce friction and heat, allowing the blade to last longer and stay cooler during cutting. Blade guides can also be bearings. Carter is a company that makes bearing guides, and theirs are the ones that I use. There are other bearing-guide companies out there, so using Carter's guides is just a suggestion. Bearing guides will give you the longest blade life.

The blade we will use for most of our cuts is a ⅛"×.025"×14-tooth regular. I have found the best blades in that size are made by Starrett. Later in the book, we will use Olson blades that are ⅛"×.018"×14-tooth regular and ³⁄₁₆"×.025"×14-tooth regular.

The ⅛"×.025"×14-tooth blade will be used for making very tight turns. When you get good with this blade it is possible to cut a hole about the size of a cigarette's diameter in 6" of soft maple. This blade is used for all lock-and-slide and interior compartmentalization cuts. The slightly thinner ⅛"×.018"×14-tooth blade is used for sliding drawers only and the ³⁄₁₆"×.025"×14-tooth blade is used for cutting off bottoms or for long, straight cuts.

STEPS 2-3   Now that we have all of the necessary equipment, it's time to tune up the band saw. Put a blade on the saw and center it on the wheel using the adjustment on the back of your saw (see your saw's manual for more specific instructions). This adjustment tilts the top wheel, which regulates the tracking of the blade. This will help you adjust the blade to track in the center of the wheels.

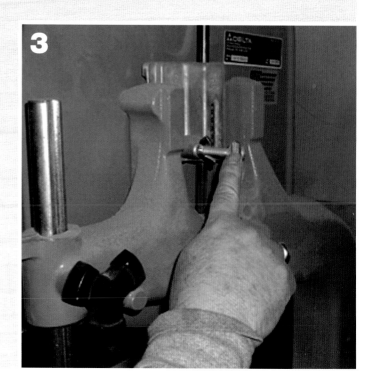

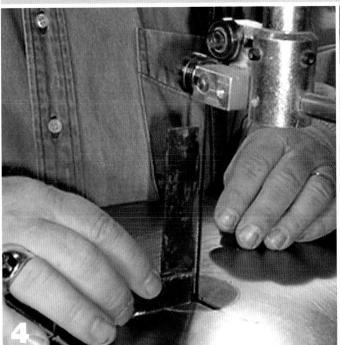

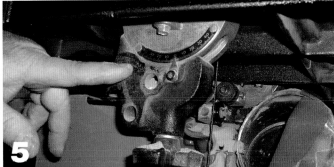

STEPS 4-6 Using a small 90° square, level the table of the saw to the blade.

STEPS 7-8 Now, set the guides as close to the blade as possible. Using the 90° square, re-check the blade to ensure that it is 90° to the saw table.

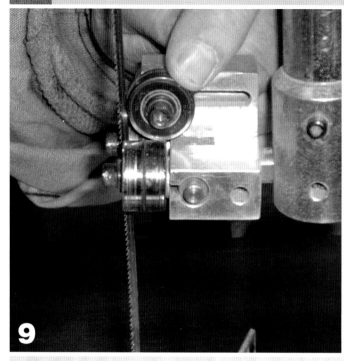

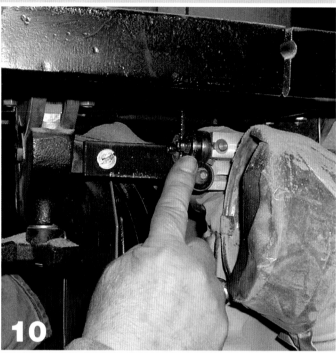

STEPS 9-10 Adjust the upper (photo 9) and lower (photo 10) thrust bearings so they *lightly* touch the back of the blade.

STEP 11 Gently hold the blade against the thrust-bearings and check to make sure that the blade is 90° relative to the bed of the saw in that direction. If you find yourself cutting a taper, one of two things is wrong. Your wood may not be 90° to the blade and/or your adjustments need to be re-checked.

STEP 12 How tightly should the saw blade be tightened? On the back of most saws is a guide for blade tensioning. Start at the point of recommended tension for your saw. If the blade is too tight, you will know it when the blade starts cutting a ridge in the tires of your band saw! If it's too loose, when cutting through thick wood, the side of the wood that the blade comes out of will not be straight. Instead, it will have what I call a "belly" to it, or a slight curve. Ultimately the blade tension for your particular saw will be found by using the saw and being attentive to what works and what doesn't.

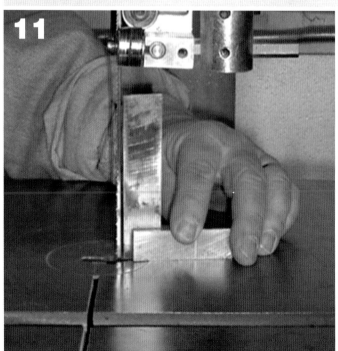

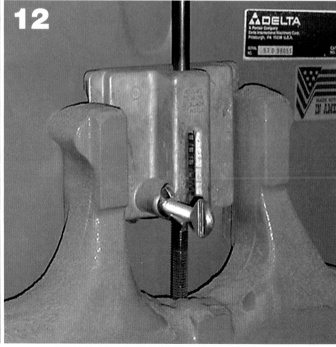

The Wood

You can use any wood that is *dry* (6% moisture content) to make a puzzle box. Remember, we are making mechanical pieces, meaning that parts will be moving and sliding. If the wood warps, the box will not work. If your wood is not dry, then you will be making the most expensive fire wood ever seen by man. I air dry my wood from three to five years before cutting it.

I have found that you can buy redwood 4×4 construction lumber that is kiln-dried. Starting out, this is the best wood to work with. It is dry, soft, relatively inexpensive and it is the right thickness for beginners. Keep in mind that the harder the wood, the harder it will be to cut, and the shorter the life of the blade. Wood may also be glued together in layers, or laminated, but should be allowed to dry for at least thirty days before cutting.

Most of my wood comes from the west coast; from John Keppinger in Oregon. California and Oregon are the places from which most burls come. The burl of the tree starts approximately 6" above ground and goes down from there.

Because the soil is so sandy, the burls on the west coast will grow to enormous sizes. This type of wood is beautiful and fun to work with. You cannot buy it dry, so you must have the patience to properly dry it before you try to make a box with it.

The challenge in working with burls is cutting long-grain and cross-grain that are intermingled. When ordering burl, you purchase by the pound rather than the board foot. (Burl is too difficult to measure in terms of board feet.)

Since you are buying wood out of the ground, it will be wet and can lose as much as 50% (buckeye, for example) of its weight in the drying process.

As you work with various woods and ask questions of your suppliers, you will soon learn the drying times of those woods. For example, I allow one year of drying time for every 2" thickness of maple. So, a 6"- thick piece of maple would require three years to dry. You will find that staying with softer woods is better for making band-saw boxes.

I once made a box from African Rosewood. It wasn't very big, but the wood was so hard that the blade was ruined by the end of that one box. If I am using a softer wood, such as soft maple, I'm usually able to cut fifteen to twenty boxes with one blade.

(photos below) When choosing wood for a box blank, the grain should be oriented so the crown is pointing up, with the grain running side-to-side as shown in the left photo. Burled wood (right photo) will yield some beautiful boxes.

Using Magnets to Conceal

Rare earth magnets are powerful and usually fairly small. There are several websites that offer a wide variety of these magnets, K&J Magnets being one of them. The standard magnets have the magnetic poles on opposite ends. There are barrel style magnets that have the poles located in each half of the magnet. This means that instead of stacking on top of each other, they will line up side-by-side.

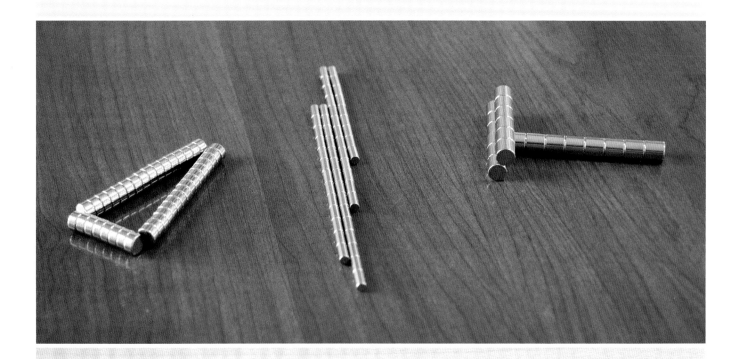

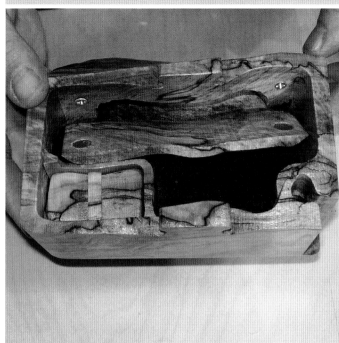

If an irregular-shaped piece of wood has a bottom larger than the top, you can cut out some material from the inside front of the box using a wood-grinding bit. Install a couple of short screws in the inside front of the box as shown above.

Drill holes on the inside of the shoulder piece and install some magnets.

(photo below)   Now you've got a clever secret compartment.

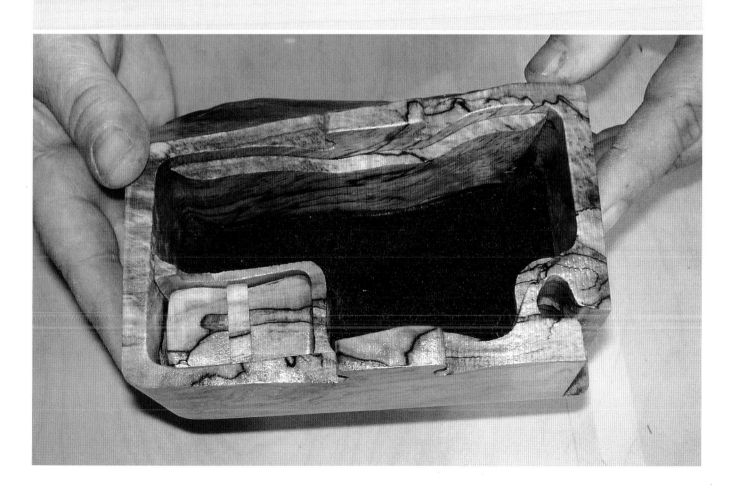

Preparing Box Blanks

I use a stationary belt sander to prepare my box blanks. (You could clamp a portable belt sander upside down in a vise.) The first thing to do is sand the blank's sides smooth. Then sand the bottom 90° to the sides. The sides of the blank will always be long grain. Round all corners and edges slightly, except for the bottom ones. (The bottom corners and edges should be left square so you will not be confused as to orientation when you start cutting. The best orientation for the wood is to have the crown at the top of the blank. Also, I have found that boxes look good when the sides are 90° to the bottom. However, the top does not have to be parallel to the bottom.) Sand to a minimum of 180 grit. This will make your finish sanding much quicker and easier.

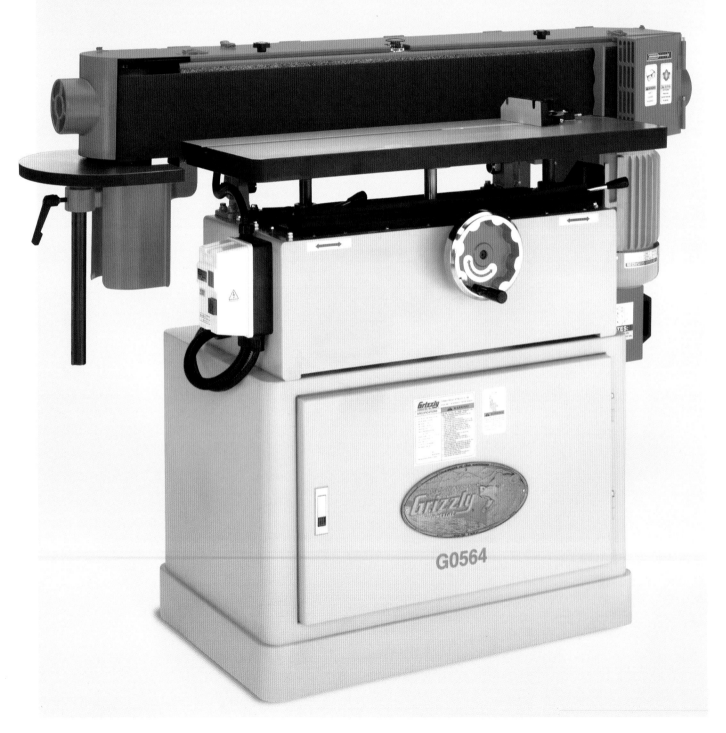

G0564

Band-Saw Practice

STEPS 1-2 Using 4×4 redwood, cut a block approximately 5" long. At each corner, draw a key with square corners as shown in photo 1. This will help guide you when cutting the keys. Then draw two lids on the side (the side being the part with the long grain). This will be your practice block to cut and then throw away.

STEPS 3-11 Adjust the upper blade guide so that it is approximately 1" above the top of the wood. Your saw should be all tuned up and ready to go (see Band Saw, page 10), so now it's time to cut! Remember, the blade only cuts on the teeth. So, when you are making tight turns, you must keep pressure on the teeth. If, when you start cutting, you notice that you are twisting the blade, back off the turn and gently wiggle the wood ever so slightly from side to side. Then continue with the turn. A little "shake and shimmy" will help you to make a tight turn. *Do not twist the blade!*

Cut the four keys, removing each one from the block of wood as you go. A good key is one that lifts out, but does not fall out the side of the block of wood. A good top cut will slide out of both sides, but will not lift off. These first cuts may not be the most attractive, but as long as they do their job, they are fine. Beauty will come with practice! Keep making these cuts until you are comfortable with the process.

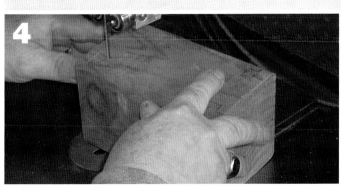

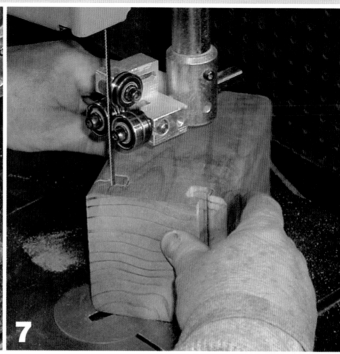

STEPS 6-9   Keep cutting keys. Cut each one as if it were to be cut square. The rounded corners happen automatically.

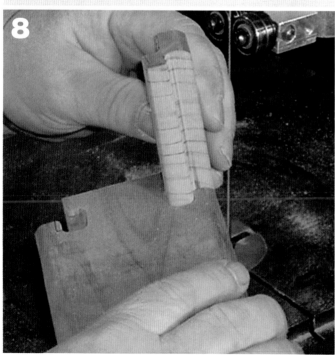

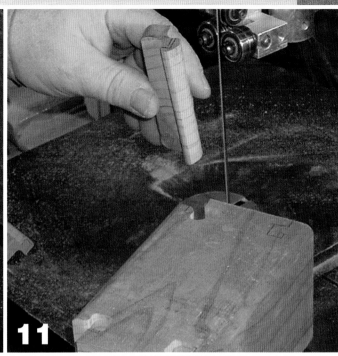

STEPS 10-13 By the time you're through cutting just these four keys, you'll be surprised at how easy it has already become for you.

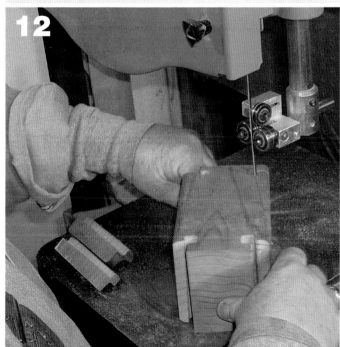

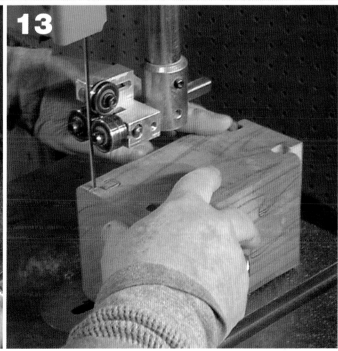

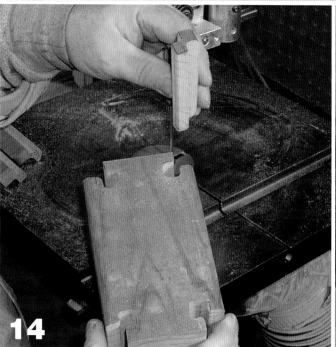

14

15

STEP 14   The last key. You are now an expert "key cutter".

STEPS 15-17   Turn the practice blank on its side and start making the lid cut. When making the inside cuts at the bottom of the dovetail, turn the blank quickly but smoothly. It's a gentle action.

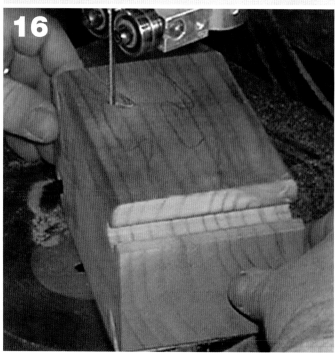

16

17

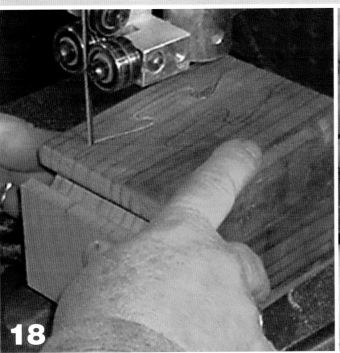

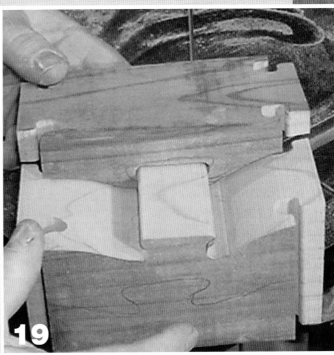

STEPS 18-21 This first cut may look a little misshapen, but never fear. Practice will make this second nature for you.

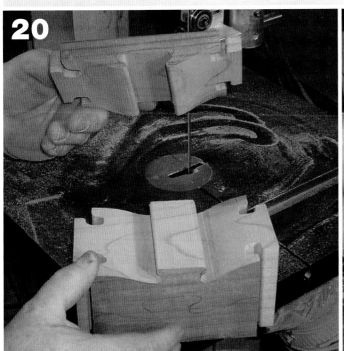

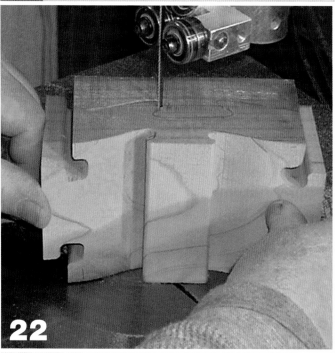

STEPS 22-25 It's impossible for you to see how smoothly I make my cuts in these step-by-step photos, but you'll know how you're doing by checking the final cut when you're finished. You should have gentle curves with minimal blade marks.

STEPS 26-29 Reassemble the blank to see how all the parts fit and lock together. If at this point you don't feel comfortable making these cuts, keep practicing. Trust me, it will get easier!

Making Our First Box

STEPS 1-2 Now let's have some fun! Make a new blank the same size as your practice blank. On the side of the blank, scribe a line parallel to and approximately ¼" up from the bottom.

STEPS 3-4 Cut off the bottom.

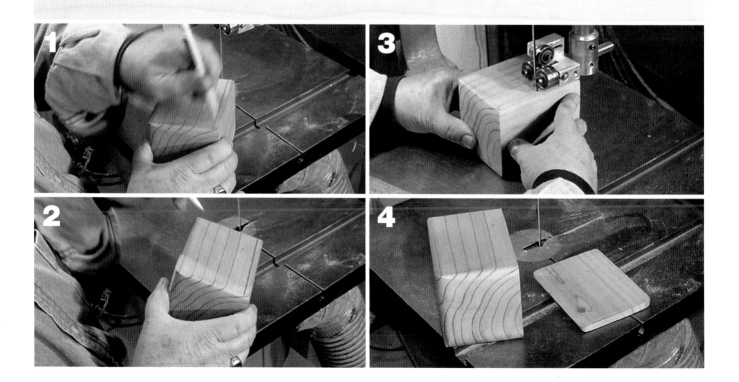

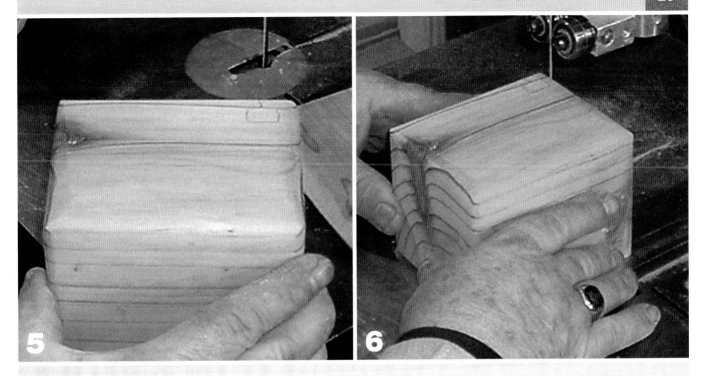

STEPS 5-9 In a corner of the top of the box blank, draw a key, cut it out and remove it.

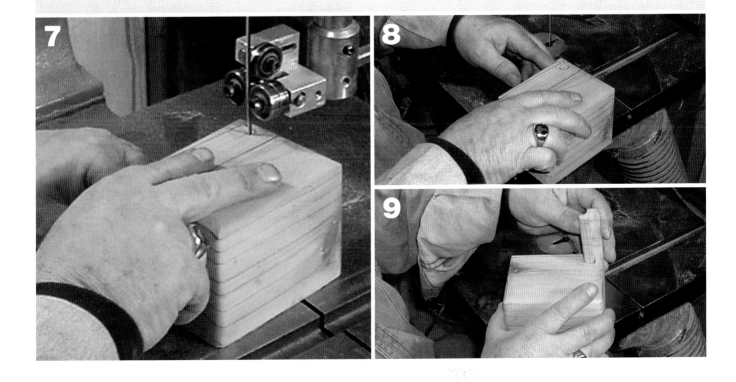

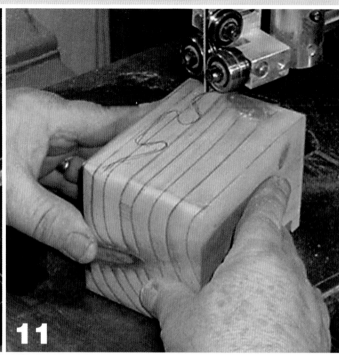

STEPS 10-13 On the side of the box, the opposite side from where you cut the key, draw a sliding lid and make the cut (the keyhole should be on the bottom of the lid). Cut the lid and slide it off of the blank.

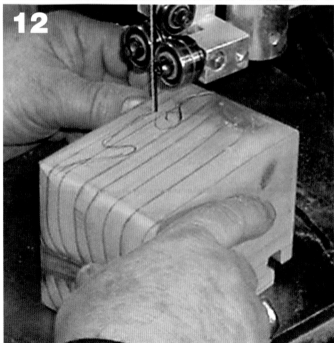

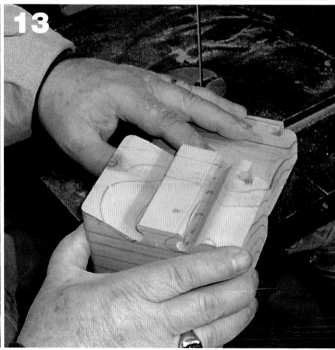

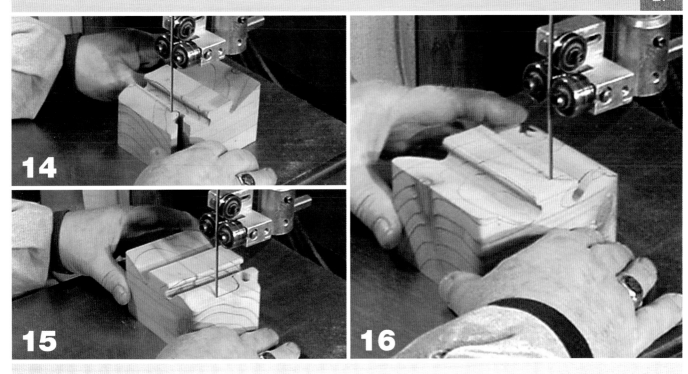

STEPS 14-19 Set the box on its bottom and cut into the box from the innermost point of the keyhole, following the outside contour of the blank. Leave the wood a little bit thicker at the dovetails where the lid slides on. This will add some strength to the dovetail. Exit the blank through the entry cut (step 18). Lift out the guts of the box and lay it on its side.

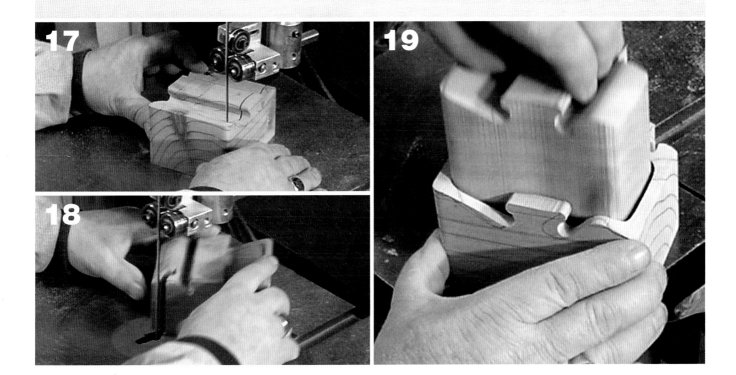

20

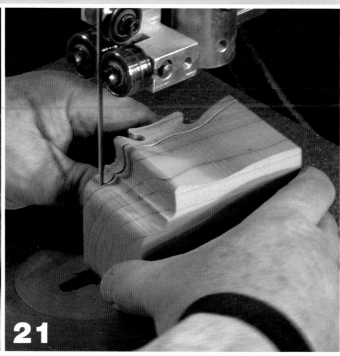

21

STEPS 20-21   Cut the top from the guts
— following the contour of its top — making it
about ¼" to ⅜" thick. Flip the remaining blank back
onto its bottom and cut what I call a "joiner". This
approximately ⅛"-thick curved piece is cut from the
corner directly behind where the key was removed,
and the entry cut was made. Later, this piece will be
glued back in place across the entry cut. Photo 23
shows the joiner laying in the background on the band
saw table.

STEPS 22-25   Starting in photo 22, cut the sides
off, tapering from 0" on both ends to ⅛" thick in
the middle.

22

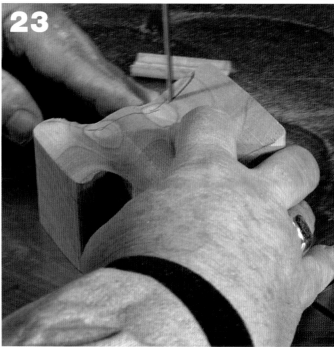

23

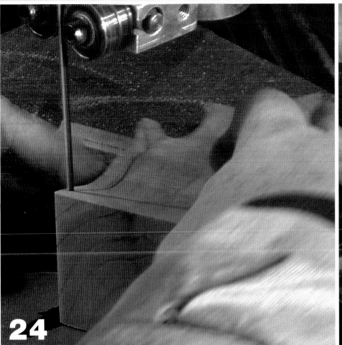

24

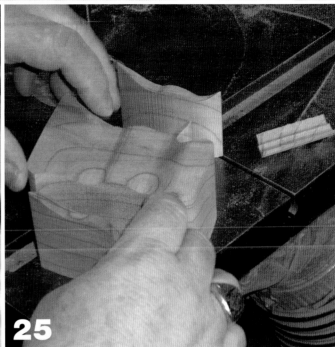

25

These tapering sides — called shoulders — will eventually be glued back in the box to support the inner, lifting lid of the box. Congratulations. You have now cut out your first box! The next steps are to sand it and glue it together.

STEPS 26-27 Put the lid on the box and orient the bottom to properly fit the box. Using 120-grit sandpaper, sand the bottom *inside* edges of the outer walls of the box.

26

27

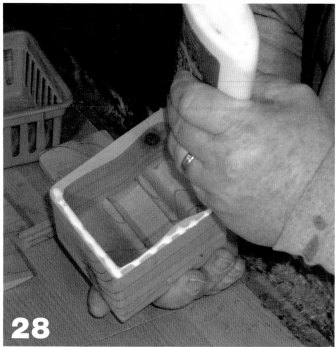

28

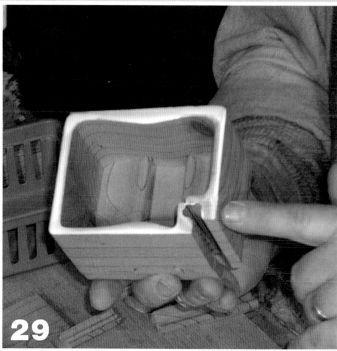

29

STEPS 28-29 I use Elmer's woodworker's glue to reassemble the box. Make the bottom edge of the box that will connect to the base wet with glue. Let the glue set for about a minute. Then, wipe off most of the glue from the inside edge, especially at the keyhole. Make sure you still have a good bead of glue on all of the outer surfaces of the bottom edge.

STEPS 30-31 Place the box onto its base and match it up to the sides. Making sure it does not move, use weights or clamps (or a combination of the two) to ensure that the wood does not slide as you let the glue dry. If you have done this correctly, you will see glue squeezing out from the sides of the box and not squeezing out on the inside of the box or keyhole. Leave the box clamped and/or weighted for at least an hour.

30

31

32

33

STEPS 32-33   Remove the weights and/or clamps. Slide off the lid and locate where the shoulders and joiner will fit back inside the box. Lightly sand the bottom edges of the shoulders and joiner so that they will sit better on the bottom of the box. Put glue on them, keeping it away from the ends and tops of the pieces. It's okay if the bottom gets glue on it, but do not intentionally put glue there as it will squeeze out.

STEPS 34-35   Put the shoulders and joiner in place along the walls of the box and clamp them with gentle clamps such as clothes pins. Let the glue dry for an hour, then remove the clamps.

At this point, the inner lid should drop into place (being supported by the shoulders) and the outer lid should slide on. The key should drop into its hole, locking the box together. You now have your first working box. Let's finish it.

34

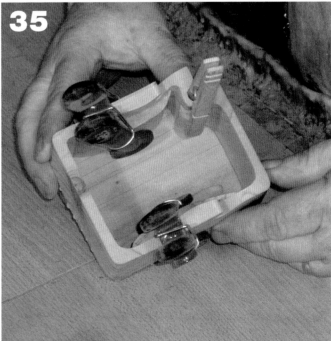

35

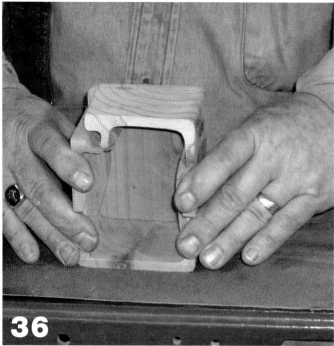

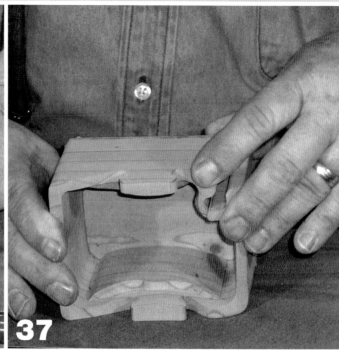

STEPS 36-39 Going back to the belt sander, disassemble the box. There should be four pieces: The body, the inner lid, the outer lid and the key. While cutting your box, you may have noticed that the side of the box where the blade came out is rougher than the side where the blade entered. This roughness is called *tear-out*. Using the belt sander, sand the side with the tear-out until all glue and tear-out is eliminated. Then sand the other side and both ends to eliminate the glue seam.

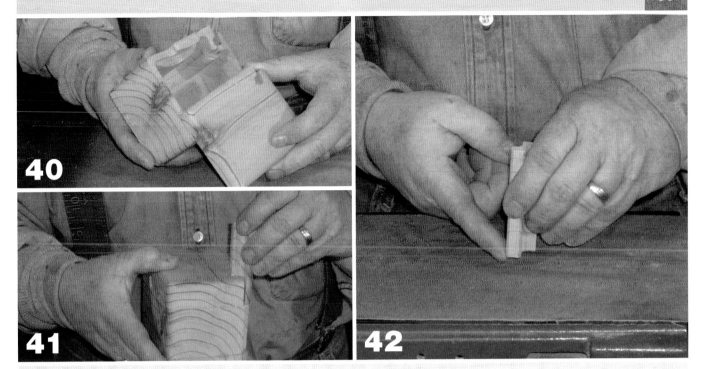

STEPS 40-44 The glue seam should be almost invisible. (If the glue seam is noticeable, the glue joint wasn't wet enough, or there wasn't enough weight or clamps on the piece.) Set the inner lid in the box and the outer lid back on the box. Having sanded the body, the outer lid will now slightly overhang the body, especially on the tear-out side. To eliminate this, line up the box and the outer lid as best as you can and sand sides of the top flush with body. Now insert the key. It will stick up above the top of the box. Carefully sand the *bottom* of the key until the top of the key matches the top of the box.

Looking down the side of the box where the key is, you may find that they key does not quite match the side. Holding the entire box together with the key in place, gently sand the side until it matches the key. Sand on the end of the box to match the other side of the key. Use the sander to re-round all of the corners. A nice, finished box has *no* hard edges — everything is rounded. Remember, use a *gentle* touch when using a power sander.

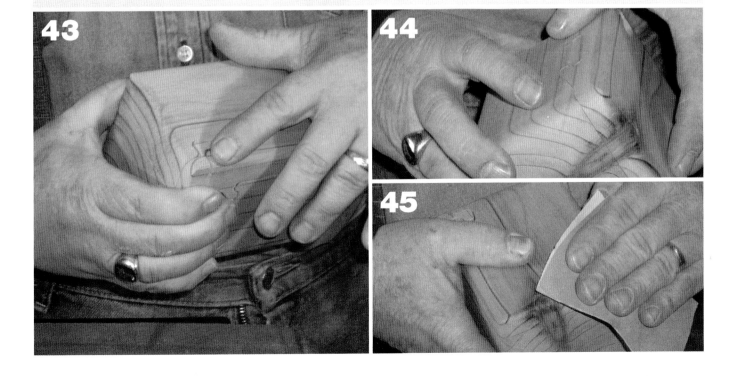

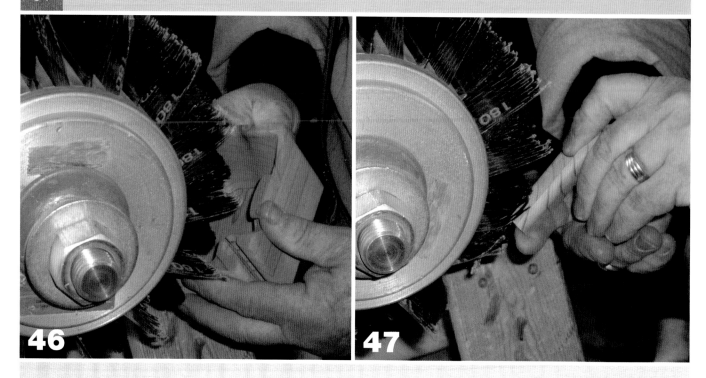

STEPS 46-49   Take the box apart again, and, using either a flapper sander or 180-grit sandpaper, gently sand the inside of the outer lid, all surfaces on the inner lid and the top edges of the box. Round all of the corner points on the outside edges of the body. Now, let the box sit for at least one day. This will allow the glue to fully cure.

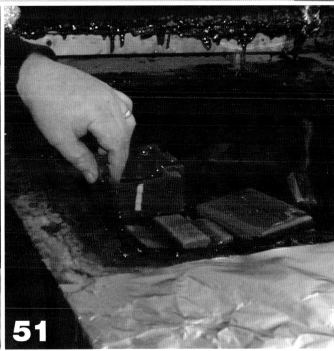

STEPS 50-53 For finishing, I use Deft's Step Saver, which is a second-generation Danish Oil that has 60% more solids than conventional Danish Oil. The Danish Oil will strengthen and stabilize the wood. This makes a huge difference in the longevity and durability of the box, especially burl-wood boxes. Soak the box parts in the oil for about two minutes, then place the parts in a drying area (such as a drip screen or on old rags) and let them dry for half an hour. Using paper towels or rags, wipe off any excess oil. *Remember: All used paper towels or rags must*

be put into a metal, fireproof container. They can and will blow up! I almost lost my shop ten years ago by not believing this could happen.

Let the oil cure for a minimum of two days. Then put a top-coat finish on it. I use Deft's Clear Wood Finish, semi-gloss, which is nitrocellulose lacquer. I spray 5-7 coats on the outside and two coats on the inside. (I spray one coat, let the finish dry and sand with 220-grit sandpaper. Then I spray two more coats, let them dry and sand with 320 grit. Finally, I spray two more coats and sand no more.)

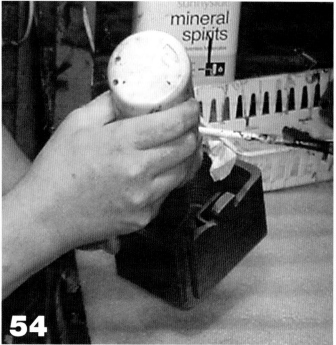

54

55

STEPS 54-59 The outside of the box is now completely finished, and it's time to finish the inside. I line my boxes with felt, using a product called Suede-Tex, which is powdered felt that can be blown into the box. It is made by the DonJer Company. Suede-Tex is available in a rainbow of colors. You purchase the powered felt and a matching color of adhesive. You will also need a duster. DonJer makes one for about $5.00.

The first step is to carefully paint the adhesive into the box. You can paint any surface to which you want the felt to stick. (Obviously, avoid painting any surface where you don't want the felt to stick. If you do get adhesive where you don't want it, it can be removed with mineral spirits before it dries.) Immediately use the duster to apply the felt powder. This process is best done within the confines of a cardboard box to limit the mess that the blowing felt will make. This should be left to dry for 24 hours. Then blow or vacuum out the excess felt.

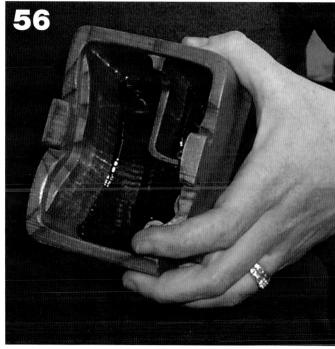

56

57

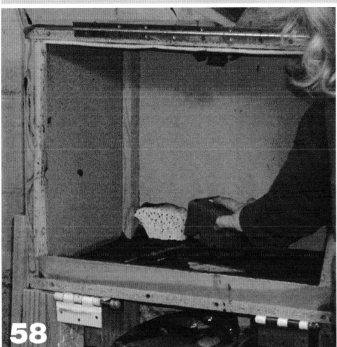

STEP 60   The final step is to put some felt feet on the bottom of the box. Felt feet are little dots of felt with adhesive on the back. (They usually come in rolled strips or sheets and can be purchased at hobby supply stores.)

STEP 61   This is your first and most basic box. As the chapters progress, you will learn to embellish the internal compartments, add puzzles and make spring-loaded drawers.

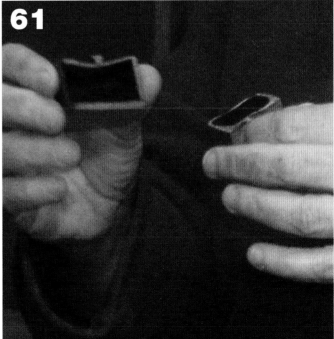

The Next Step Up

STEPS 1-2 Cut a 4×4 redwood blank approximately 7" long. Prepare the blank, cut off the bottom and cut the first key.

STEPS 3-4 When I make a box that is over 6" long I always make two separate, locking lids. The reason for this is to prevent the lid from warping. (Shorter lids have less of a chance to warp.) In the box we just made on the preceding pages, the

dovetail cut to make the outer lid creates a handle for you to lift out the inner lid. When you cut off the top for *this* box, we want to create an upside-down dovetail (opposite from the shape in the previous box) that will leave a slot in the blank. So, cut the first lid (about 4" long) using an upside-down dovetail (step 4). Remove the lid.

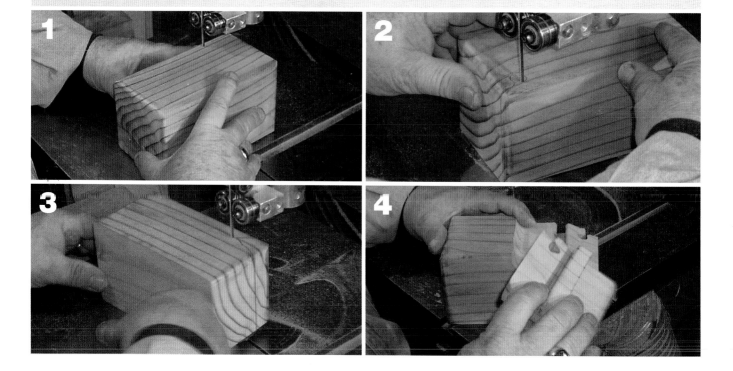

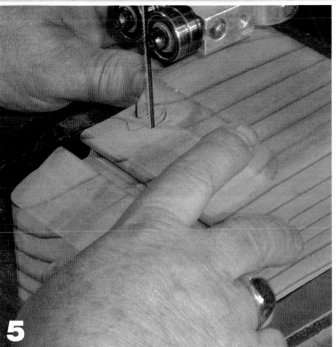

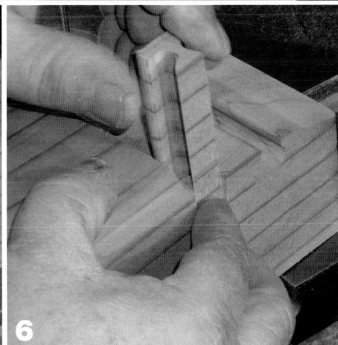

STEPS 5-6 Cut the second key into the side of the box so that the first lid will cover it when replaced. Cut the key as close to the end of the first lid as possible, then remove the key.

STEPS 7-10 Lay the box on its side and start the cut in the hole made by the second key. Cut at the center of the hole and then turn the cut to create the second lid that copies the upside-down dovetail shape of the first lid.

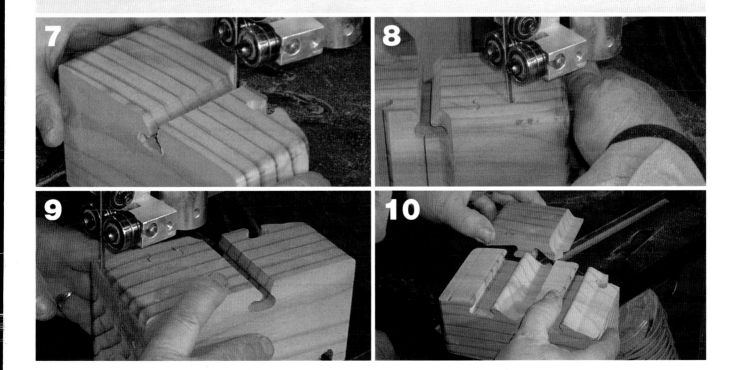

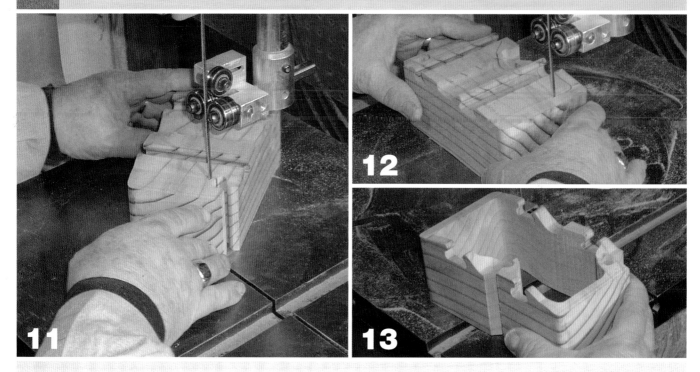

STEPS 11-13 With the two lids removed, put the box back on its bottom, cut into the box through the first keyhole and hollow out the box. To strengthen the walls, leave a little extra thickness in them around the key slots for the second lid.

STEP 14 Remove the inside guts and cut off its top to make the inner lid.

STEP 15 Before cutting the shoulders and joiner, cut the framework for a smaller inner box to sit inside the main compartment. There are no measurements here — it doesn't matter how big you make the inner box. As a general rule, cut it approximately ¾" × 1½". Draw a small rounded rectangle onto the wood. This rectangle needs to connect on two different sides of the box (see photos 18 & 19). Flare the ends so you will have no square corners where these ends meet the inner sides of the main box. Draw a ¼" frame around the rectangle as shown.

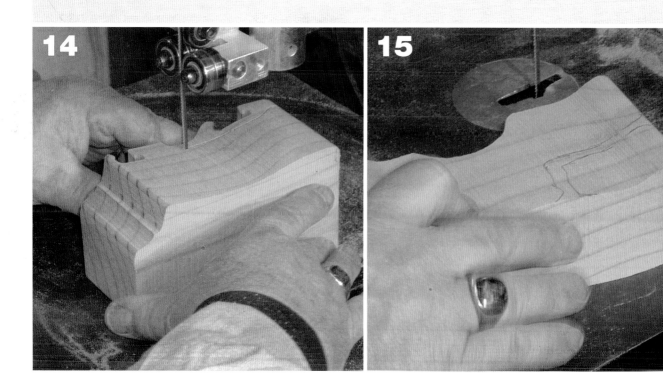

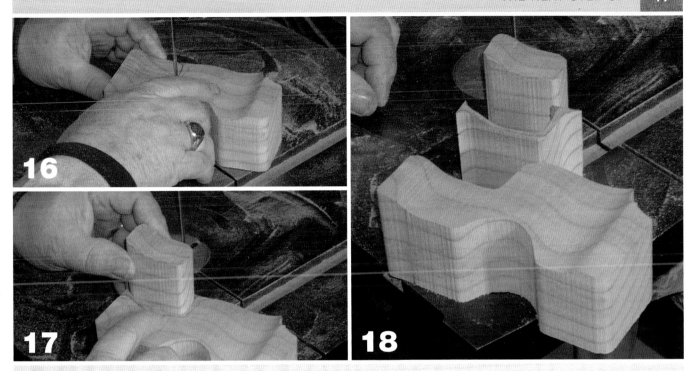

STEPS 16-19 Cut out the rounded rectangle and side pieces and set them aside.

STEP 20 Now cut out the shoulders and joiner.

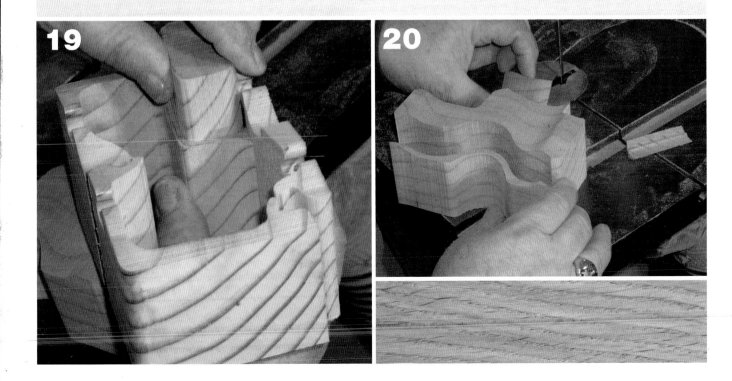

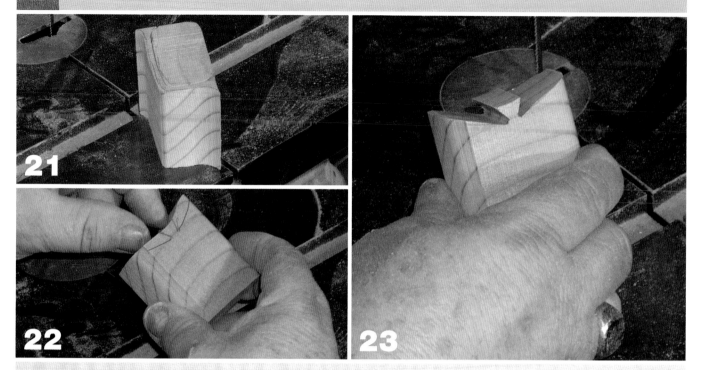

STEPS 21-23 Go back to the small rectangle (this is a small inner box) and cut a small dovetail on its top. This is a handle for the box.

STEPS 24-27 Draw two lines on the side of the box, one approximately ⅛" up from the bottom and one approximately ¼" down from the top. Holding the handle, cut off the bottom and then the top.

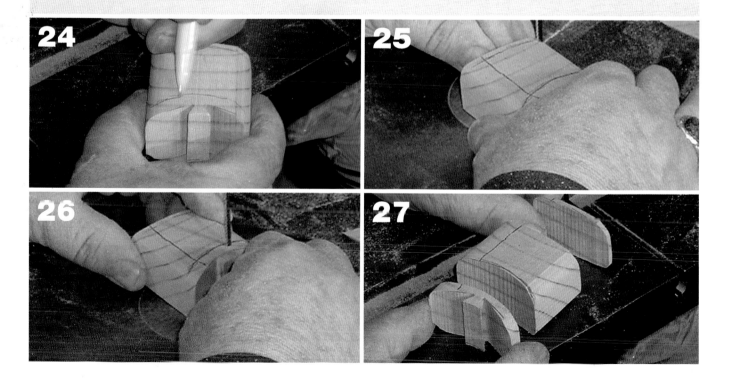

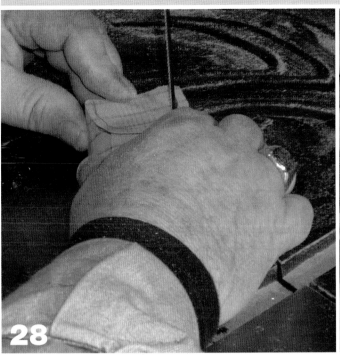

STEPS 28-29 Setting the top and bottom aside, draw a line around three sides of the box. This will be a drawer. Cut it out and set the framework of the box aside. What is left will become a drawer inside the inner box.

STEPS 30-32 Cut a dovetail to use as a handle in the side of the drawer. Now cut off the bottom of the drawer, approximately ⅛" thick.

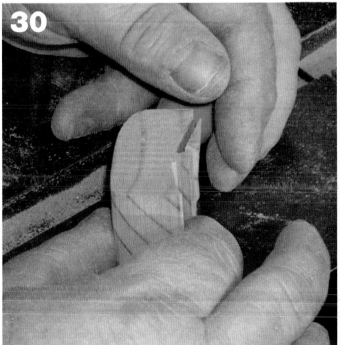

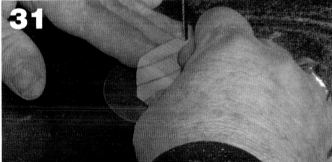

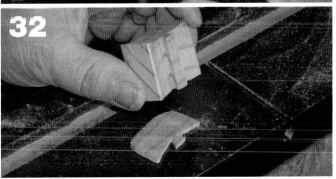

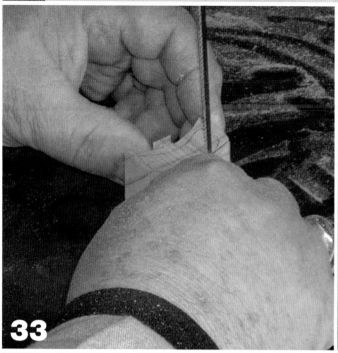

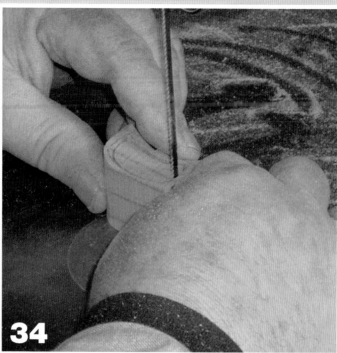

STEPS 33-35   Cut in from one corner and hollow out the inside of the drawer, leaving the edges as thin as possible. When you come back to where you started the cut, make a small flange, or rounded corner, that overlaps the first cut. This gives you a place to clamp the joint when gluing the drawer back together. Now carefully back the blade out.

STEP 36   De-bur the bottom edges of the body of the box.

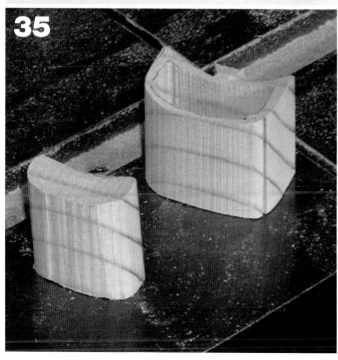

STEPS 37-38 Put the lids back on the main box and glue the bottom on the box.

STEP 39-41 Glue the front and back onto the small inner box and clamp it.

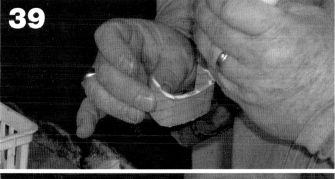

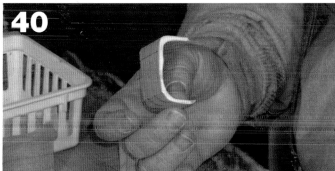

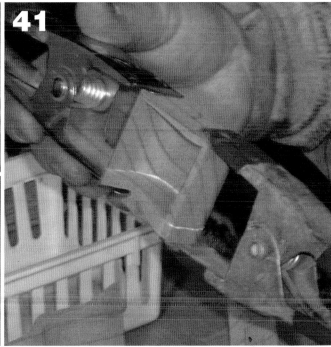

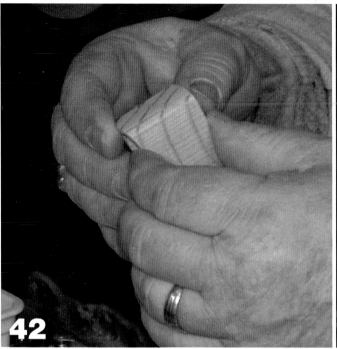

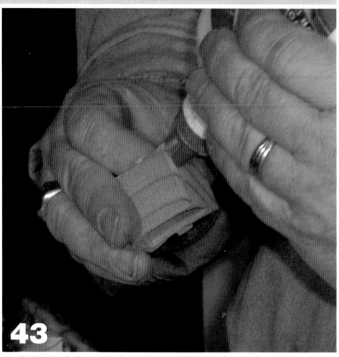

STEPS 42-45   Apply glue to the seam of the small drawer and clamp it.

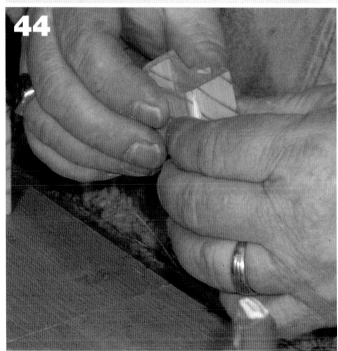

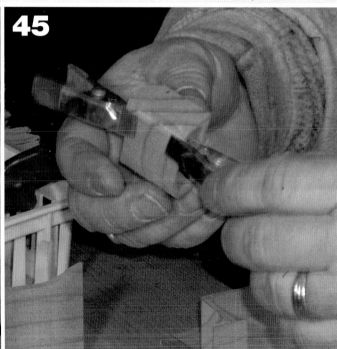

46

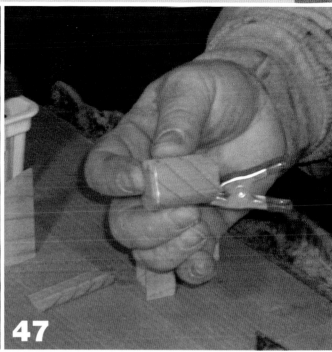

47

STEPS 46-47 Next, glue the bottom of the small drawer onto the body of the drawer.

STEP 48 The framework for your inner box should be lightly sanded on the top and bottom. Where the frame meets the walls of the body, sand a small bevel on the bottom corners. This way, if any glue is stuck on the inside corners, the framework will still fit tightly. Place the small inner box in the corner and use it as a guide to

position the framework. Put glue on the bottom and sides of the framework and then wipe most of it off. Put this framework in place without sliding it along the side or back of the main box. Remove the inner box so that it doesn't get glued in place accidentally.

STEP 49 Glue the shoulders and joiner into the main box. Let the glue dry for 24 hours. Then sand and finish the entire box.

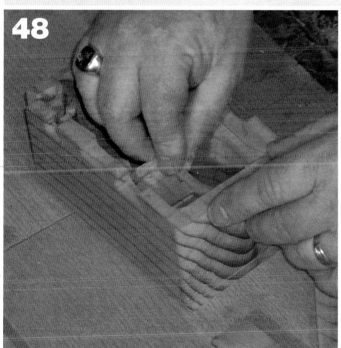

48

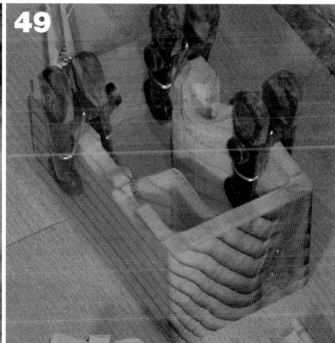

49

SECTION
TWO

49 The King's Safe

68 Box in a Log

82 Round-Drawer Spring Box

96 Two-Drawer Spring Safe

118 Holes are Cool

126 Ultimate Jewelry Box

THE KING'S SAFE

It's time for you to try your hand at making a more intricate piece — The King's Safe. It's a fun-to-make, coffee-table conversation piece or a great box for that youngster who has "cool stuff" he or she wants to keep safely hidden. We're talking about things like notes from a friend or that neat-looking rock they found.

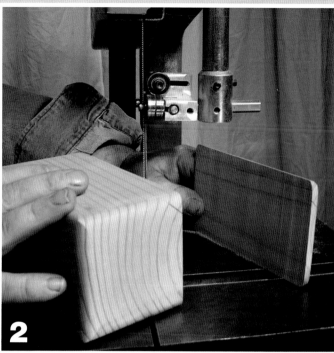

STEPS 1-2 This project will use many of the steps we've already discussed (and practiced). This blank is about $3\frac{1}{2}$" × $3\frac{1}{2}$" × 6" after it is sized and sanded. Cut off a bottom approximately $\frac{1}{4}$" thick.

STEPS 3-4 Cut the first key.

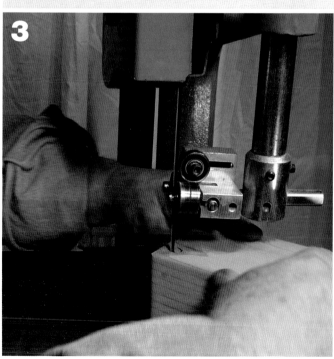

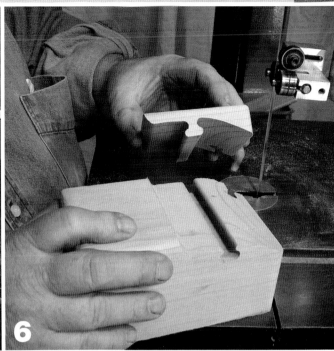

STEPS 5-6 Cut out the first lid.

STEPS 7-8 Make a large, sweeping dovetail through the lid.

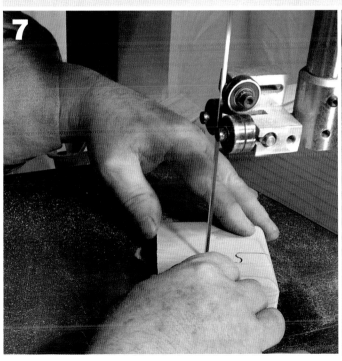

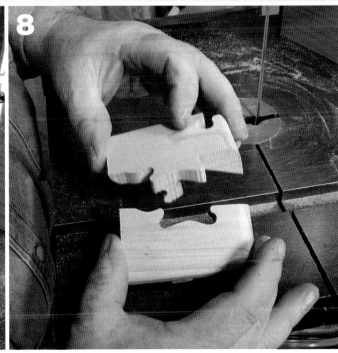

STEPS 9-10   Orient the box with the keyhole in the upper left corner. Cut another dovetail key in the upper right-hand corner.

STEPS 11-12   This next cut is similar to cutting the lid; it's just a thicker piece and doesn't go as far back. Cut into the wood about ½" down from the top of the block and form a dovetail below the level of the lid's corner dovetails and slightly before the dovetail cut in Step 5.

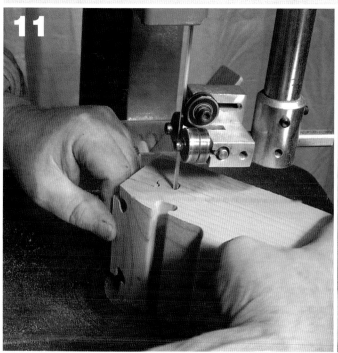

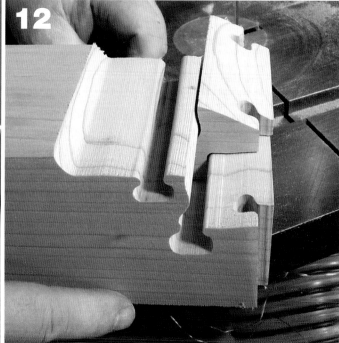

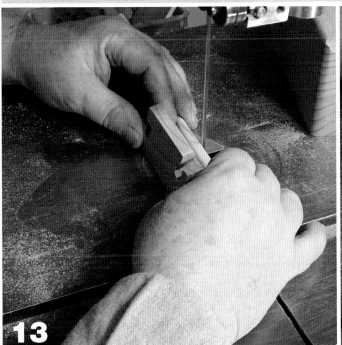

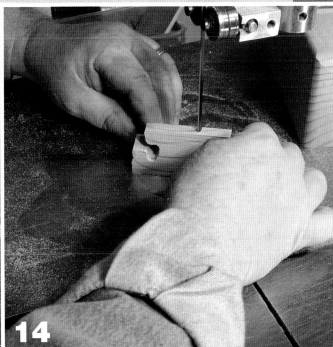

STEPS 13-15 Remove the piece you just cut and lay it on its back so the keyholes are in the up position and the flat side is facing you. Cut a dovetail so the tail part is mostly in the grooved part of the piece.

STEPS 16-18 Set the box on its bottom. Entering between the two existing keyholes, cut another dovetail key, entering the wood about the same depth as the other keyholes. Don't cut into the wood farther than the existing holes.

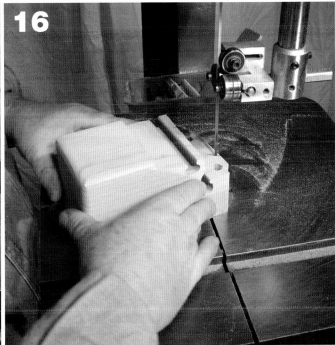

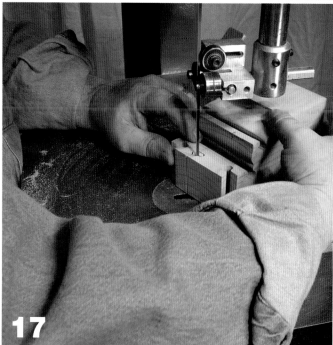

STEPS 16-18 *(continued)*

STEP 19-21 Set the box on its side so the bottom is to the right and the keyholes are facing the blade. Center the cut roughly between the bottom and the cut top surface. Cut another

dovetail like the one in steps 11-12 — without cutting off the groove from that dovetail in steps 11-12. Study the photos before making the cut.

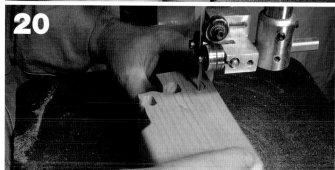

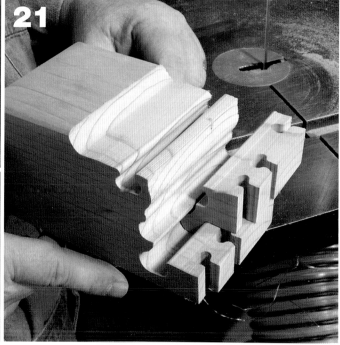

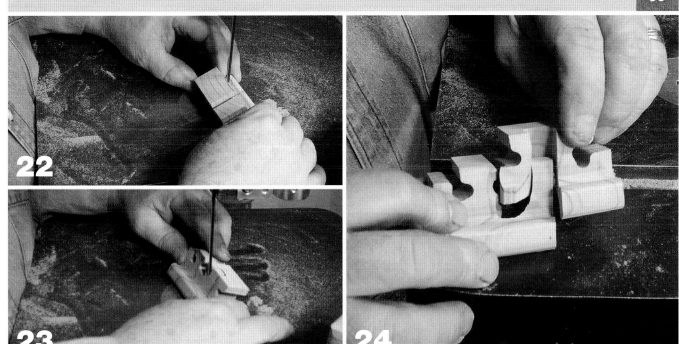

STEPS 22-24 Cut a dovetail in the center of the piece you just cut.

STEPS 25-26 With the box on its bottom, cut between the left and middle keyholes. Make the cut straight through to the dovetail groove in the lid's cut. Turn the box and come back out. The piece should be about the same width from front to back, with a slight narrowing in the middle.

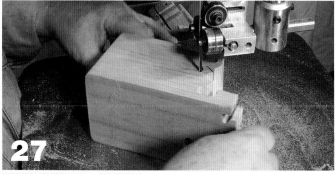

27

28

29

STEPS 27-29 Make a cut above and behind the pieces cut in steps 11-12 and 19-21, creating another dovetail. Stay about 1" away from the back swoop of the lid's cut.

STEPS 30-33 With the bottom of the box on the table, enter the opening next to the keyhole on the right. Cut in all the way to, but not through the lid's cutout. Cut only through surfaces that have already been cut. This piece should look like an elongated teardrop.

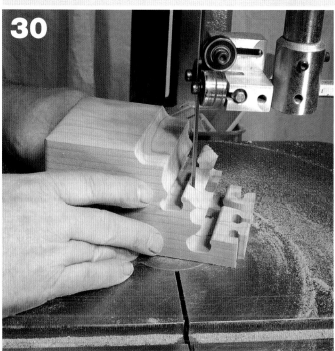

30

31

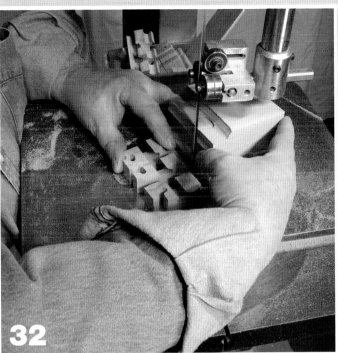

32

33

STEPS 34-37 To cut the second half of the lid, lay the box on its side with the bottom to your right and the other cuts facing the saw blade. Start cutting about ¼" below the uppermost cut surface. Arch the cut down and towards the back of the box about 1". Start the dovetail here so it is centered in the back portion of the box. Don't come down too far into the box — only about ¾".

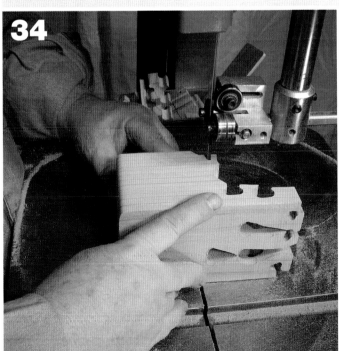

34

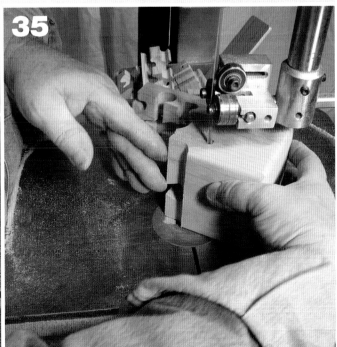

35

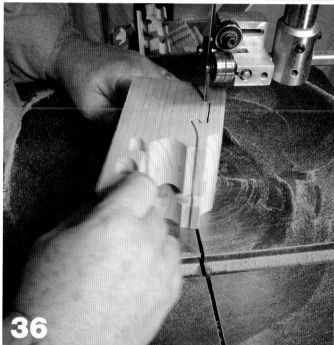

36

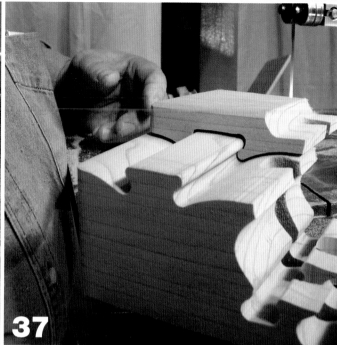

37

Continue the cut to the back of the box, making sure to arch the cut a little as it sweeps up and comes out the end of the box.

STEPS 38-40 Place the box on its base and cut out the guts. Enter through the keyhole cut made in Steps 30-33. Leave about a ¼"-thick rim around the three sides and exit through the keyhole cut. Remove the guts.

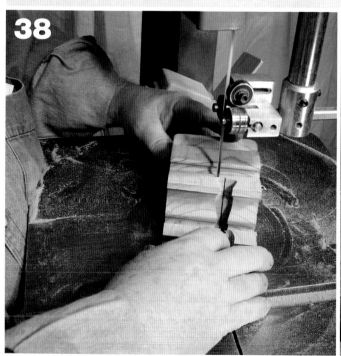

38

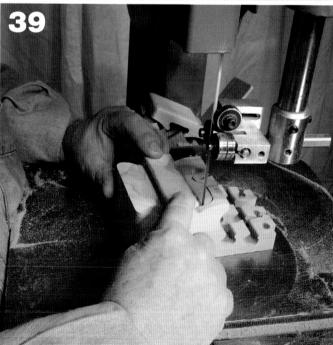

39

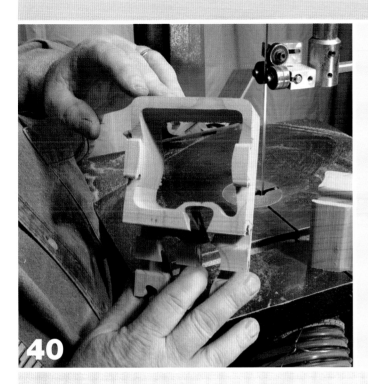

40

THICKER AT THE DOVETAILS

When cutting the guts out of a box, leave the sides a little thicker at the dovetails in the top of the box. This extra material reinforces the dovetails.

Some folks who are unfamiliar with these boxes have been known to try lifting or prying the lid off before they knew they should slide it off. Dovetails have been broken as a result. But the extra wood gives the dovetails the strength they need to withstand the force of "prying hands".

STEPS 41-42   Cut a lid from the guts.

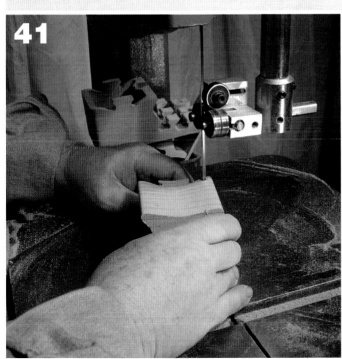

41

42

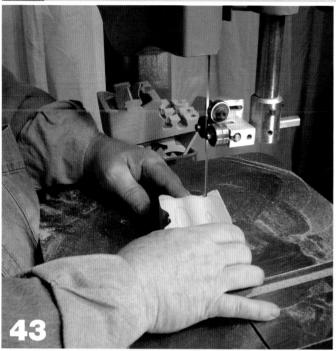

STEPS 43-46   Cut the shoulders from the left and right sides of the remaining guts.

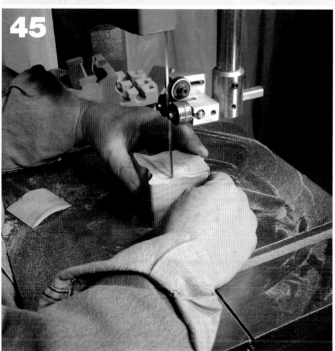

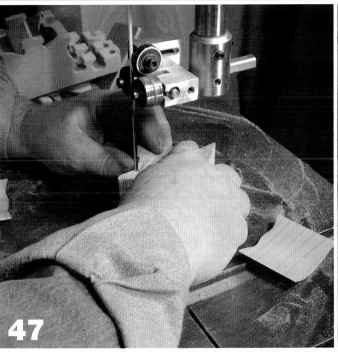

STEP 47 Cut the joiner from the corner of the guts at the point of entry through the keyhole.

STEP 48 You should have a lid and three pieces cut from the guts.

STEP 49 Here's all the parts for the box. As you can see, this box is another step up in puzzle box construction.

STEP 50 Sand the burrs from the base of the box. You are not trying for a smooth finish, just getting rid of the stringy stuff that keeps you from having a good glue joint.

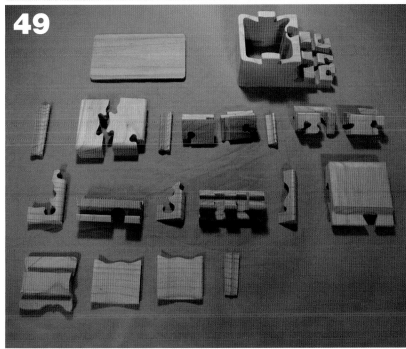

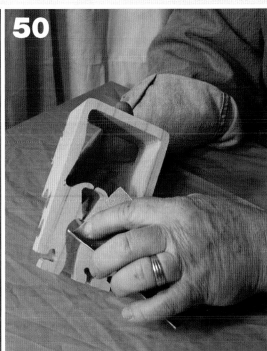

51

52

STEPS 51-52 Apply some glue and smear it to an even coating.

STEPS 53-54 As before, remove some glue, leaving only enough so the wood is wet but not slick, leaving a thick bead of glue around the outer edges. This will help create an almost invisible glue joint.

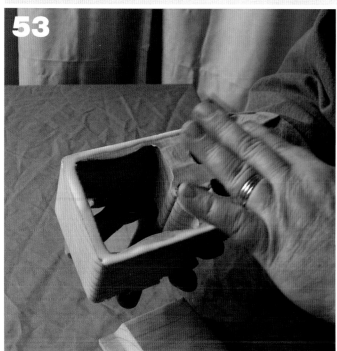

53

54

55

56

STEP 55 Using the wood grain as a guide, match the bottom with the base.

STEP 56 Put the lid on the box and set the box on a flat surface with the puzzle side overhanging. Apply weight to the top of the lid and make sure the box does not slide on the base. Get it into place before the glue starts setting.

STEP 57 Use spring clamps to hold the base in place on the puzzle end.

STEP 58 After the glue has dried, check for any glue that may have seeped out into the dovetail cuts.

57

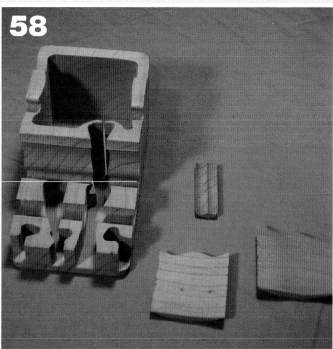

58

59

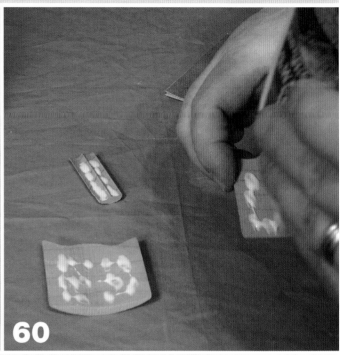

60

STEP 59 Lightly sand the shoulder and joiner pieces to remove the burrs.

STEPS 60-62 Add glue, put the joiner in place and hold it using a clothespin.

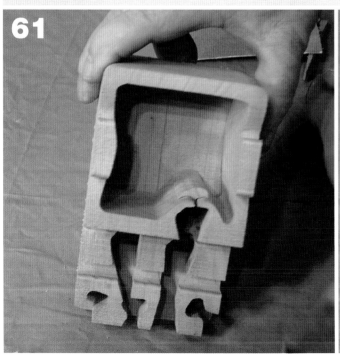

61

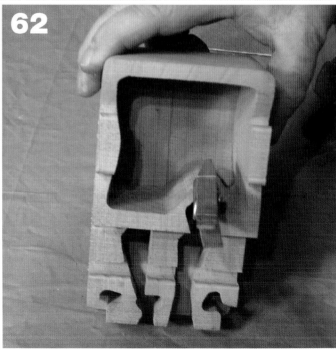

62

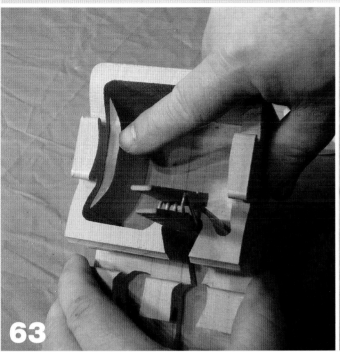

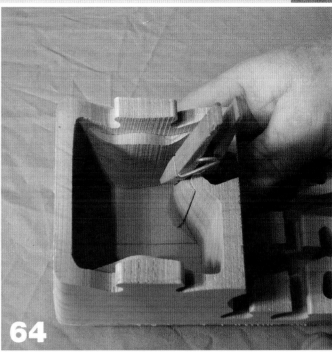

STEPS 63-64 Now glue the shoulders in place. Use clothespins or small spring clamps to hold them in place until the glue sets up.

STEPS 65-66 When the glue has set up for 24 hours, use a belt sander with 180-grit sandpaper to smooth the glue joint. Be sure to keep the box flat on the surface so you don't round over the edges. Sand all four sides.

STEPS 67-68 *Gently* sand parts that have rough edges.

STEPS 69-70 Use a flapper sander to smooth the inside edges of the box.

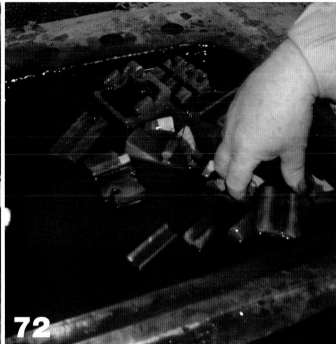

STEPS 71-72 Pour some Deft's Step Saver into a container and drop all the box pieces into the oil. Move them around and make sure all areas get covered. Let them soak for several minutes.

STEPS 73-74 Remove the parts from the oil finish and let the finish drain off the parts. After 30 minutes, rub the excess oil off the parts. Let the parts sit for few days or until the oil finish has dried. Then apply at least three and up to seven top coats of lacquer.

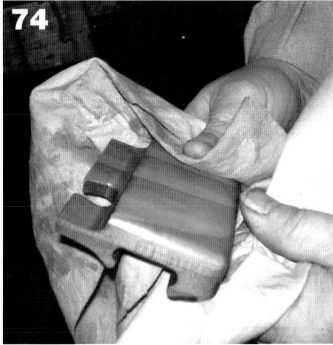

BOX
IN A LOG

Years ago a friend gave me a bunch of cedar logs from his farm. As you know, when logs dry they usually end up splitting. I looked at this wood for many years, attempting to figure out how to cut it into a box utilizing the split. Here's what I finally did.

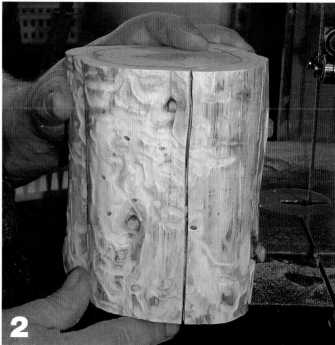

STEPS 1-3 Cut off a piece of log that is approximately 6" tall. Clean off the bark and sand the ends of the log, making them as flat and square to the sides as possible. Lay the log on its side and rotate it until the top is parallel with the blade. Then cut a ½"-thick slab off the top of the log.

STEPS 4-8 Now turn the log upright, and, using the crack as an entry point, cut in approximately ½".

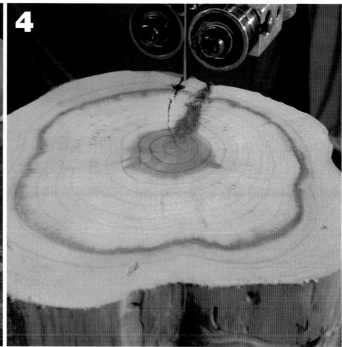

Then make a U-turn (you're making a cut that will function like a dovetail cut) and cut back towards the outside of the log. Cut around the log following the contour, leaving the wood at least ¼" thick until you reach halfway around the log. Turn and make a cut the same way you did at the crack. Remove this piece.

STEP 9   Turn the log on its side and cut off a bottom that is approximately ½" thick.

STEPS 10-12   Once again, turn the log upright, and, cutting in through the crack (see arrow, step 11) approximately ¼", make another U-turn cut and follow around the uncut side of the log until you get to the notch left by the removal of the first half of the log. Cut around that notch approximately ⅛" wide, following its contour. Exit the wood on the other side of the notch and remove that piece.

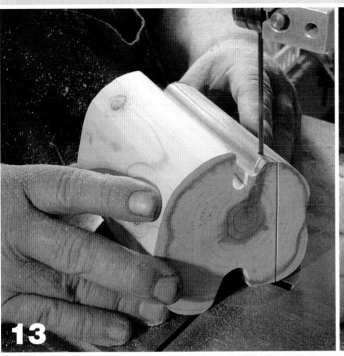

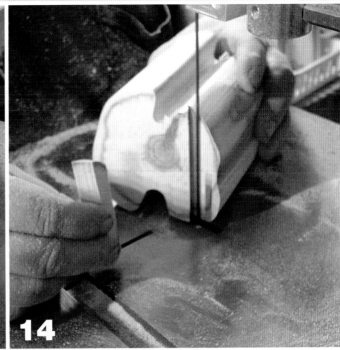

STEPS 13-15 The center core that is left will now be cut into a normal lock-and-slide box. Making notch cuts from both sides, cut a handle in the top.

STEPS 16-17 Next, cut off the bottom. I find that the handle you've just cut makes a great place to hold and steady the box as you cut away the bottom.

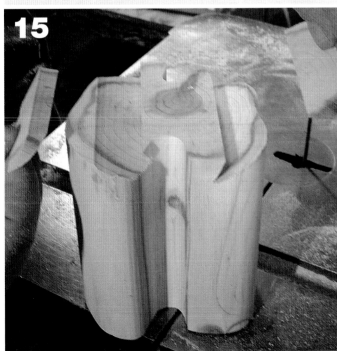

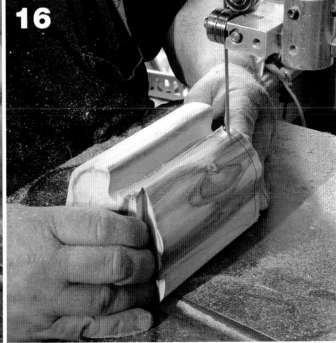

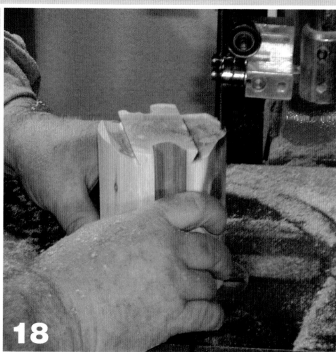

STEP 17 *(continued)*   Removing the bottom
from the guts.

STEPS 18-20   Cut a key from the side.

STEPS 21-22 Cut off the top.

STEPS 23-25 Cut in through the split to hollow-out the box. Remove the insides.

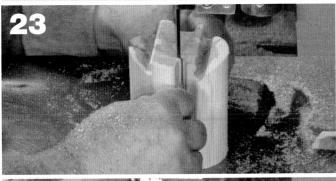

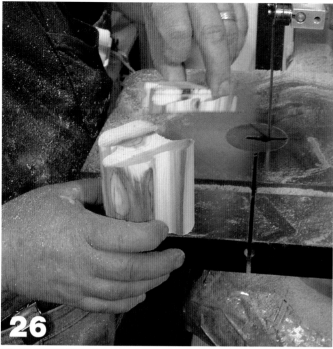

STEP 26 Cut off the lid from the inside piece. This cut doesn't need to be straight across, so follow the shape of the handle to add some flair.

STEPS 27-30 The secret to making this box stable is to seal the crack. The joiner that seals the crack will also be part of the framework for a smaller, inner box. This wall will incorporate the

crack within it. Draw the wall beginning on one side of the crack, going in till the the crack ends. Then make a 90° turn to cross over to the edge of the box. Draw a parallel line on the other side of the crack (photos 27 & 28). Now make the cuts, following the lines you just drew. Remember to round the entry and exit points so they blend with the sides of the box (photo 29). The arrow in photo 30 points out the completed wall.

30

31

STEP 31 With the guts from the inside of the "wall" you can make another little box. But this piece is actually too tall and thin to allow easy access to the new box, so I first cut away the center of the wall leaving the crack end tall (photo 32 & 33). When the wall is glued back into the box, the tall side will join the box together on both sides of the crack.

STEPS 32-33 To make the little box a better size, I cut it shorter, to the height of the inner wall, and then notch the top to create the handle for the box.

32

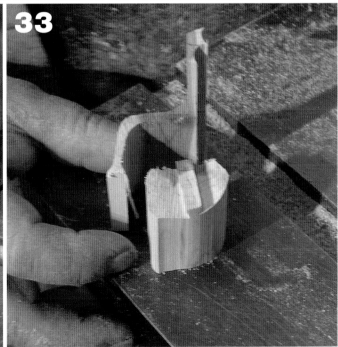

33

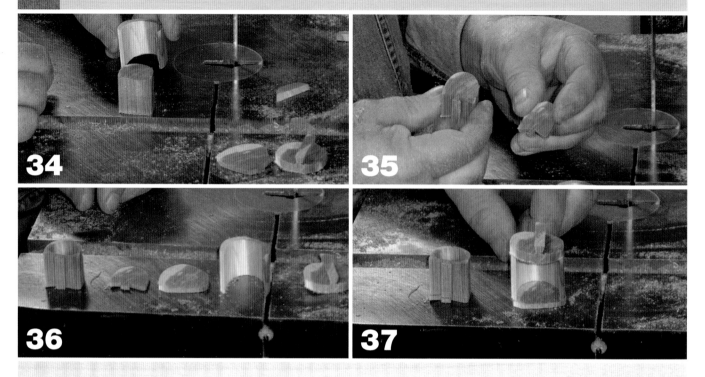

STEP 34   The inner box will have a drawer accessed from the side, so cut the lid and bottom as you would on any other box. Then follow around the inside of the remaining guts to form the drawer.

STEPS 35-37   Cut the handle on the front of the drawer, then cut off the bottom. Then cut an access slot at the back of the drawer and hollow out the guts.

STEPS 38-39   Heading back to the original box, cut the shoulders from the remaining guts.

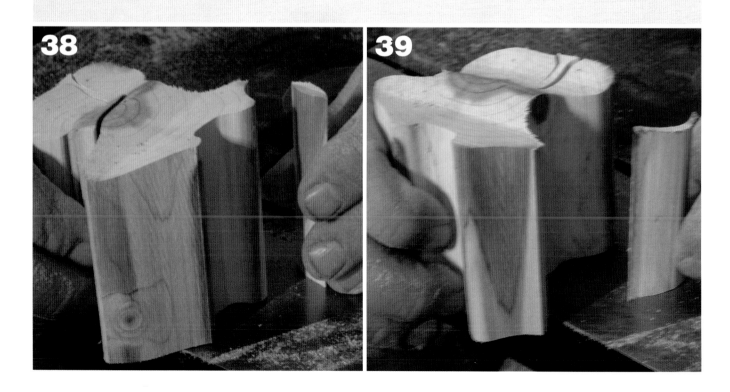

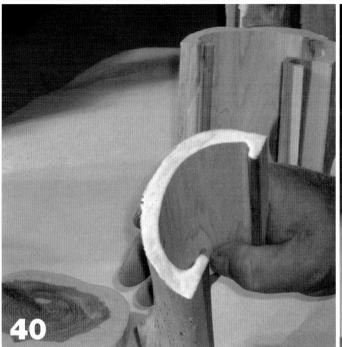

STEPS 40-41 De-bur the outer halves, top and bottom. Glue the top to the half that was cut first and the bottom to the half that was cut second.

STEPS 42-43 Glue the bottom on the inner box.

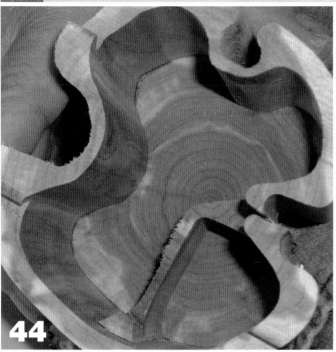

STEP 44   Glue the wall in place.

STEPS 45-47   Once the glue has dried, sand the glue joints and sand the box parts smooth and flush with each other.

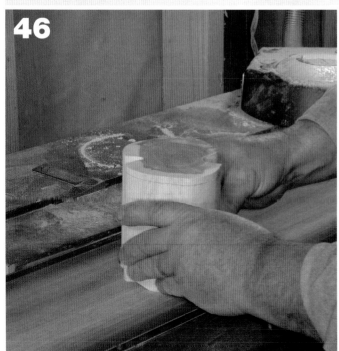

STEPS 48-49 Put the box together and round over the top and bottom edges. To finish this cedar box — go directly to lacquer — no oil sealer is necessary.

USING AROMATIC CEDAR

By its very name, you could assume, rightly so, that aromatic cedar has a pleasant smell. Making puzzle boxes from this wood gives you some options that other woods don't.

Aromatic cedar has been used for centuries for making chests, armoires, dressers and closets. Its smell, coupled with chemicals contained in the wood, repels insects; specifically moths. Clothing that is stored in cedar-lined closets, drawers and chests is protected from the moths that like to munch on wool and other fabrics. The clothing will also pick up the strong, sweetly pungent smell of the cedar.

What has this to do with puzzle boxes? Well, when you get to the finishing stage of making some cedar boxes, try leaving the insides of the boxes unfinished. This will allow the aroma emanating from the wood to scent whatever may be stored in the box. This is a nice option to have. With this in mind, you could design your cedar puzzle boxes to store small handkerchiefs or other items that would pick up the scent of the cedar.

The boxes could also simply be opened up occasionally to let the wood's odor drift into a room.

Note: Aromatic cedar can cause allergic reactions, so wear a mask when cutting the wood.

ROUND-DRAWER SPRING BOX

The round-drawer spring box is a puzzle box on top of a spring-loaded drawer. You'll be challenged to create a layered box that will give you further insight into the world of puzzle boxes. As you can see here, spalted maple makes an attractive box. Enjoy!

STEPS 1-4 On the side of the 4x4, 6"-long box blank, draw three horizontal lines. The first line is approximately ¼" from the bottom of the blank. Draw the second line about 1" from the bottom of the blank and the third about ¼" above the second line. Draw a fourth line down that intersects these three lines. This line will help you orient the parts at assembly time. Cut the three horizontal lines as straight as possible.

Cut a dovetail key from one corner of the thick top piece. Then cut a lid from the top piece that runs the length of the box and has a sliding dovetail about ⅔ in from the end you have chosen as the back. Enter through the dovetail key and cut out the guts.

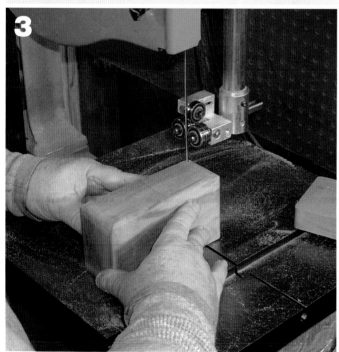

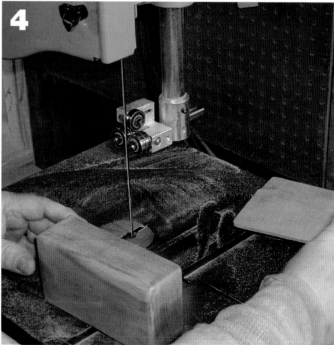

5

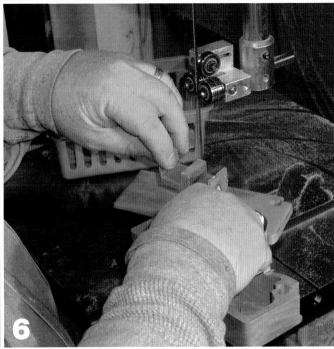

6

STEPS 5-6 Cut out a corner from the guts. This compartment conceals a key that locks and unlocks the sprint-loaded drawer. To make this key, cut out the framework wall as you would for a small inner box. Pull the block of wood from inside the framework.

STEPS 7-8 Cut off the top of the piece to make a small lid. Turn the leftover piece on its side. Begin at the center and mark off 1/8" on either side of the center point. Cut inward from these points until you reach approximately 3/16" from the bottom. Back the blade out and make a parallel cut 1/8" in from each end. Now cut out the wood on either side of the center between each of those sets of parallel cuts. Study the photos to help you visualize the cuts. Set these pieces aside for the moment.

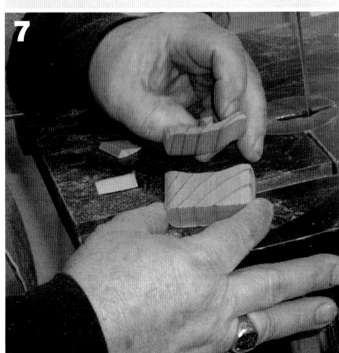

7

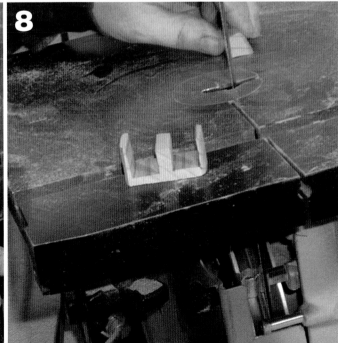

8

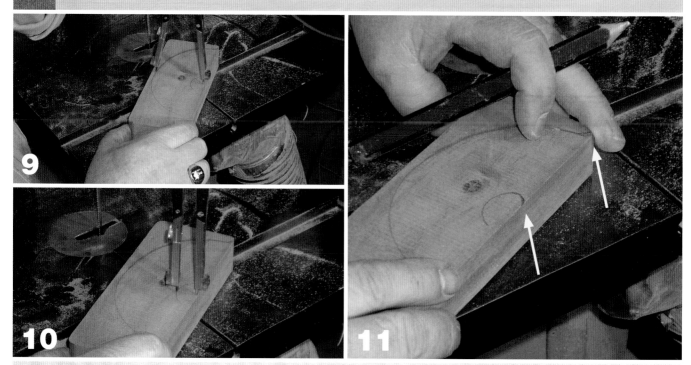

STEPS 9-11 Turn your attention back to the bottom 1"-thick piece of wood. Identify the side where the key and the little compartment from the upper section will be located. Using a compass, draw a semi circle as large as the wood will allow. Draw it so the drawer will exit beneath the small divided compartment above it. Then draw a concentric semi circle that is about ¾" in diameter. Where the drawer comes out of the wood, make a flare that creates a lip (see step 11).

STEPS 12-13 Up until now we've been using an ⅛" × .025" × 14T blade. To cut an inner drawer like this one, you need to use an ⅛" × .020" × 14T blade. This thinner blade will not make turns that are as tight as the thicker blade, but the kerf is smaller, allowing the drawer to fit better. Cut out the drawer. The arm shown in step 13 (see arrow) is a drawer stop and the "bulge" on the end of the arm is the pivot for the drawer.

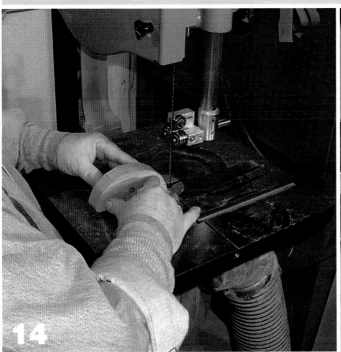

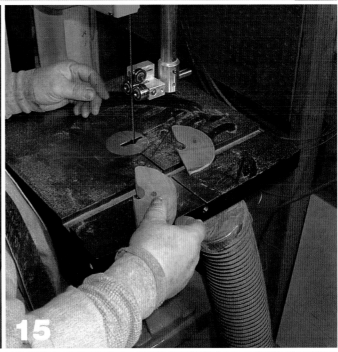

STEPS 14-15   Make the drawer bottom about ⅛" thick.

STEP 16   Cut a small sliver from the back of the drawer that tapers from an ⅛" to 0", with the thicker part beginning at the outer semi circle and the thinner part at the inner semi circle. This allows relief for the drawer to fit snugly into the box, concealing the drawer so it is not easily seen.

STEP 17   With the bottom held back in place on the drawer, the missing sliver is shown more easily. The extended bottom is a drawer guide that can be carefully sanded to provide a perfect fit of the drawer in the box.

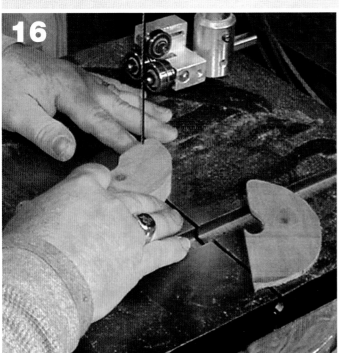

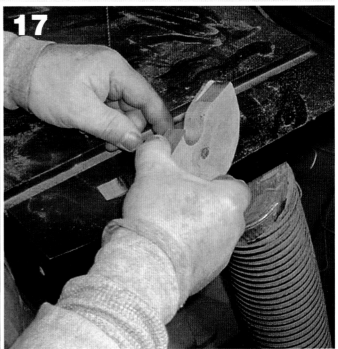

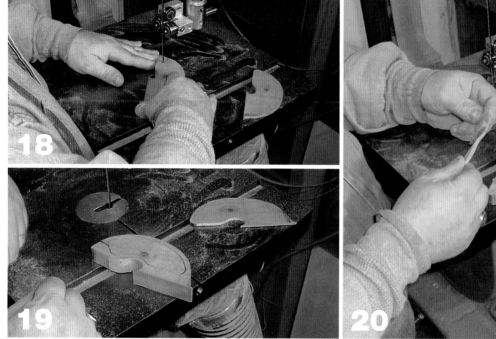

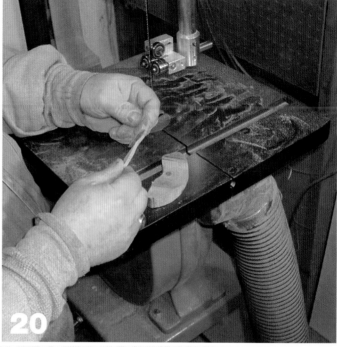

STEPS 18-20 Cut out the inside of the drawer, starting at the back of the drawer and, leaving the back about ½" thick, tapering down to follow the small inner curve and tapering again to leave the wood ½" thick at the outer face of the drawer, continuing around the rest of the curve at ⅛" thick. Remember to leave a tapered lip at the end of this cut so that you have something to clamp onto when gluing. Back the blade out carefully. Remove the center of the drawer and cut a handle into the top. Cut this top off to make the lift-out lid.

STEPS 21-22 Cut the two shoulders for the drawer to hold up the lift-out lid.

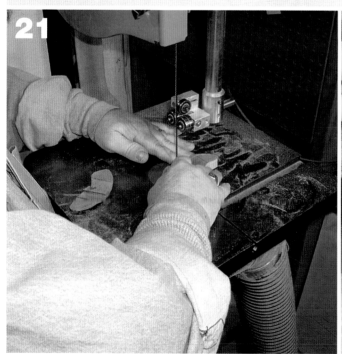

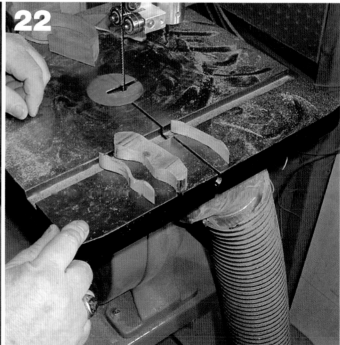

STEPS 23-24 Remove the burrs and glue the bottom onto the box. Add weights.

STEPS 25-26 Before gluing the bottom onto the drawer section, sand the outer radii of the semi circle where the drawer will insert into the box. Remove just the saw marks to reduce friction, letting the drawer slide in and out smoothly. Now glue the bottom onto the drawer section, again wiping to avoid glue squeeze out inside the box.

27

28

STEPS 27-28 Fit the bottom on the box, and add spring clamps to hold the bottom in place.

STEPS 29-30 When the glue has set up, sand the top of the bottom section and the bottom of the top section of the box until the saw lines are gone (see arrows in step 29). Apply glue, position them together, line them up perfectly and add weights. Make sure no glue squeezes out into the cavity that the drawer will slide into. It will be very difficult to remove any glue squeeze out once the box is assembled.

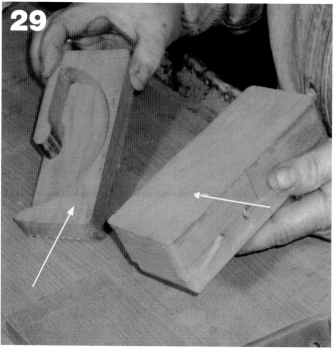

29

30

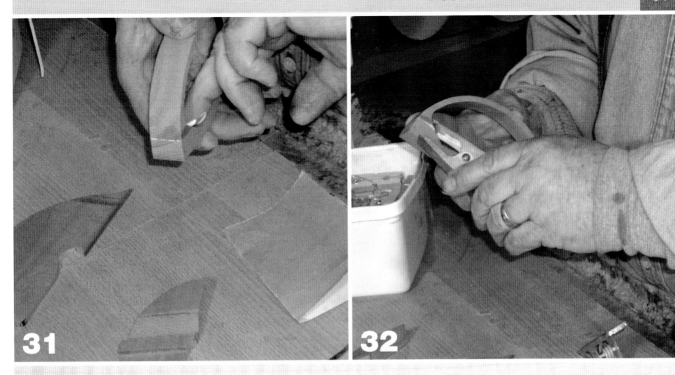

STEPS 31-32 Glue the drawer seam, again adding spring clamps to hold the joint closed.

STEPS 33-34 Glue the bottom on the drawer. Then, double check the placement of the shoulders in the drawer by inserting the lid into the drawer, making sure it seats properly. Glue the shoulders in place.

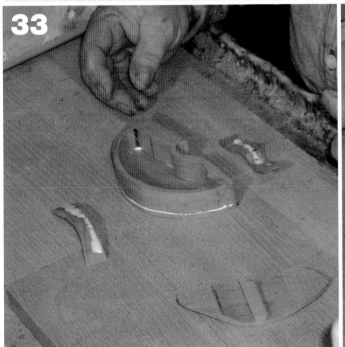

35

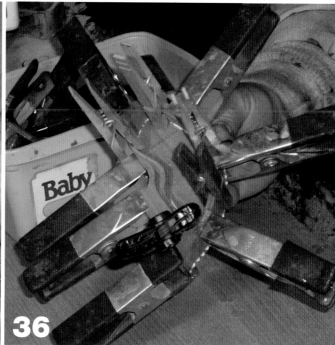

36

STEPS 35-36 Hold the shoulders in place using clothes pins.

STEP 37 Inside the top section of the box, glue the framework for the drawer-release key and the shoulders in place.

STEPS 38-39 Sand the box seams using a stationary belt sander. Sand the rounded edges (that I'm pointing to with my fingers) of the drawer using a spindle sander. Fit the drawer to its opening in the box. If needed, sand lightly on the bottom of the drawer so it will slide smoothly into the box. Don't change the contour of the drawer bottom where it meets the outside of the box. You want the drawer to be as "invisible" as possible.

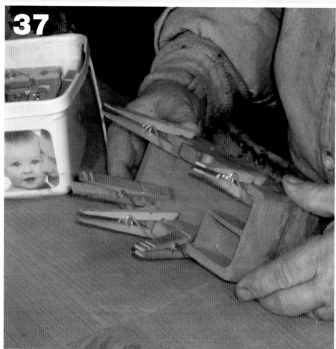

37

38

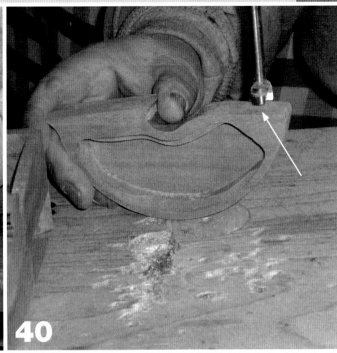

STEPS 40-42 In the back of the drawer, where the wood was left thick, drill a ½" hole about ⅜" deep for the spring. (You can find the spring [mine is a #186] or a similar one at your local hardware store.) Temporarily insert the spring into the hole.

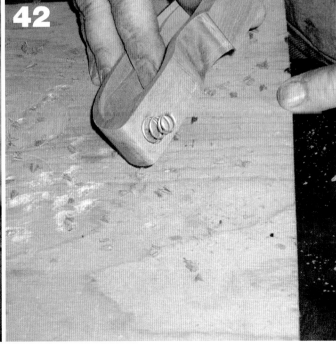

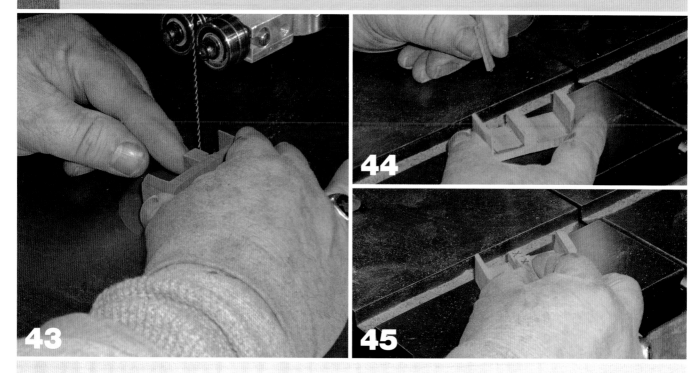

STEPS 43-45 Back to the divider key cut in Step 8. Cut a thin sliver off the top of the middle, vertical leg of the divider. This sliver is thin, but save it.

STEPS 46-48 Insert the divider key into its framework. Insert the drawer (with the spring) into the box. While holding the drawer closed as tightly as possible (photo 47), drill a ⅛" hole through the divider, the bottom of the upper section and into the drawer in the bottom section. *Don't drill through the bottom of the drawer!*

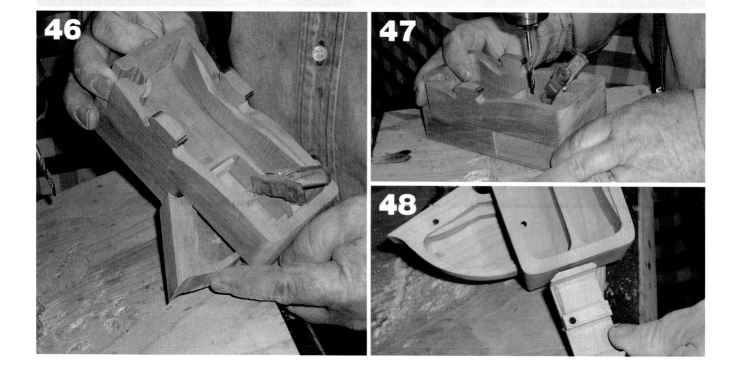

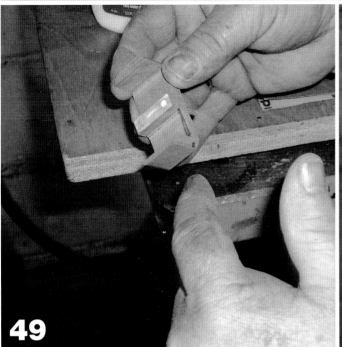

49

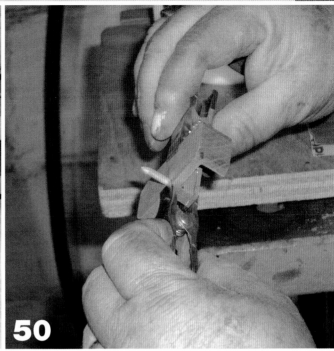

50

STEPS 49-51 Cut a ⅛" dowel about 1" long and sand one end to a point. Put glue into the hole and on the top of the center finger of the divider. Insert the flat end of the dowel into the hole from the bottom of the divider, add the sliver of wood from Step 43 and clamp it in place.

STEP 52 With the spring in the drawer, insert the drawer into the box and push the pin and divider into place, which will lock the drawer in place. The drawer front will probably be recessed a little from the face of the box. Sand the box's face until it is flush with the drawer's face. Put the lid on the box and sand the box until all the parts are flush. Do any touchup sanding and finish the box. Then, glue the coil spring into place using a little dab of hot glue.

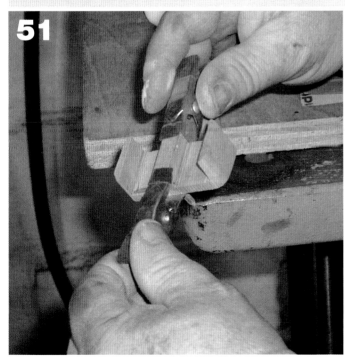

51

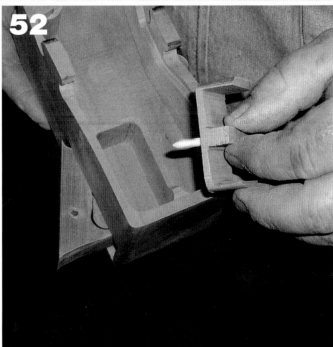

52

TWO-DRAWER
SPRING
SAFE

This box is a combination of everything you have learned so far, plus a few new things. We start with a puzzle like the King's Safe and make box with a release like the Round-Drawer Spring. Now we add another drawer that is hidden by the by the spring-loaded drawer.

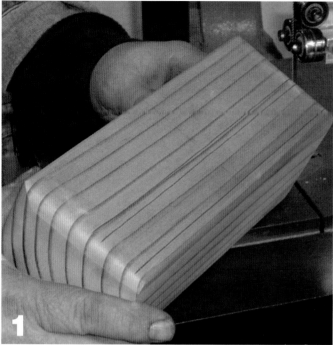

STEPS 1-2 This box is made from 4×4 redwood that is about 9" long. Once the blank has been prepared, draw lines on it just as you did on the Round Drawer Spring box. Then determine which end of the blank the drawers will spring from. Once this is decided, go to the middle line and draw a slight curve upward almost to the next line (step 2).

STEPS 3-4 Cut the blank into four horizontal pieces, following the lines. Start with the bottom. Then cut out the next level (which will be the spring drawer). Follow the curved line at the end of the drawer when making this cut (step 4).

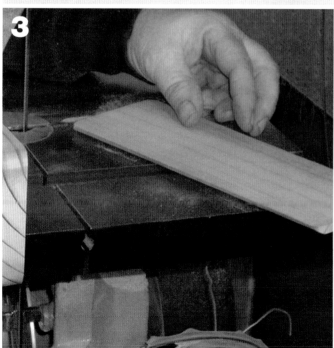

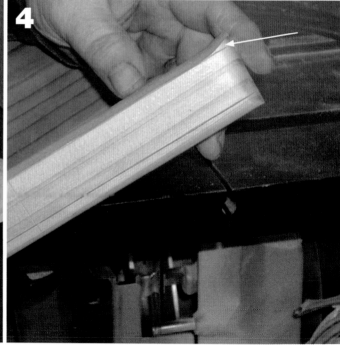

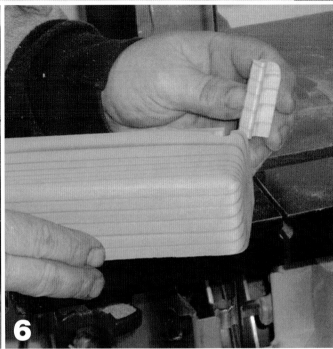

STEPS 5-6 With the four horizontal pieces cut, take the thickest top piece and cut out a key in the left corner. Cut a puzzle like the King's Safe, but this one is only one level deep.

STEPS 7-8 Then turn the box on its side and cut out a top, (with an inverted dovetail) about one-third the length of the box.

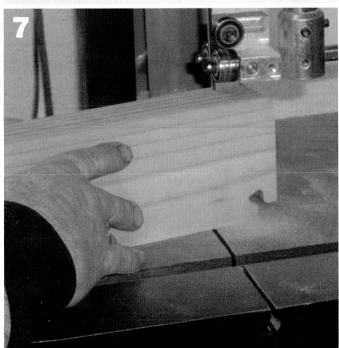

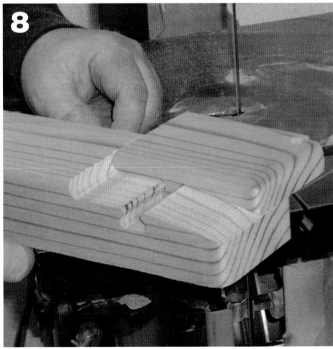

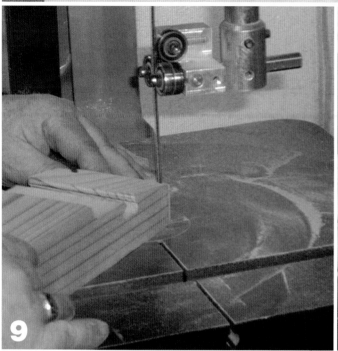

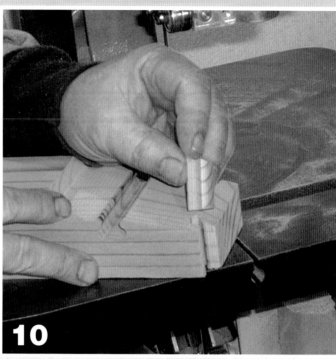

STEPS 9-10   Return to the top section and cut another key on the other corner of the box.

STEPS 11-12   Again, turn the box on its side and cut out a sliding piece with a dovetail, stopping the piece short of the dovetail from the first cut, and just below that dovetail (photo 12).

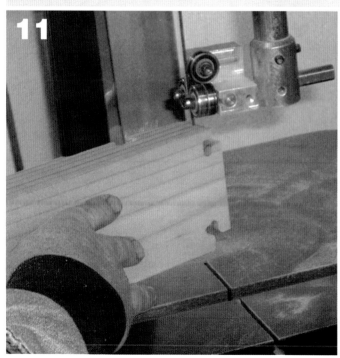

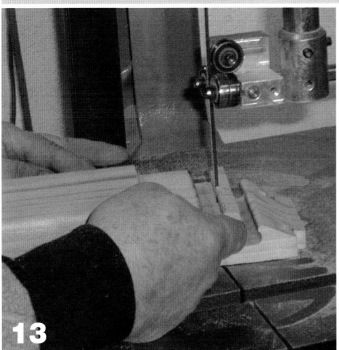

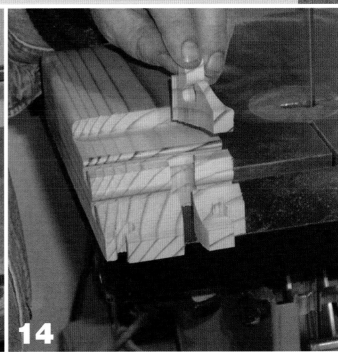

STEPS 13-14 Next, cut another key that extends deeper into the box, as shown above.

STEPS 15-16 Then flip the box back on its side and cut another sliding piece that surrounds the dovetail groove created during the first cut (photo 16).

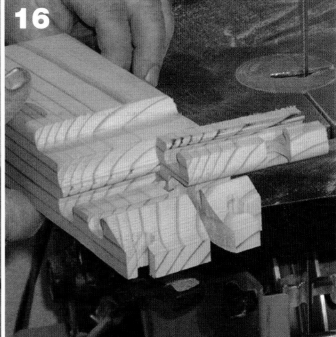

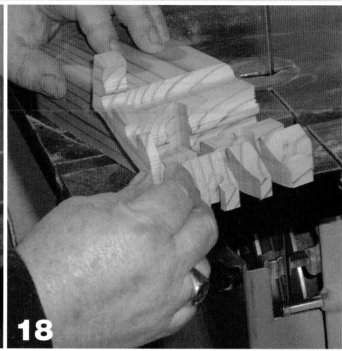

STEPS 17-18 Cut another, even longer, key that extends back just short of where the first top stopped, located to the left of the last key (photo 18).

STEPS 19-20 With the box back on its side, cut a top out of the remaining two-thirds of the box. This time use a right-side-up dovetail.

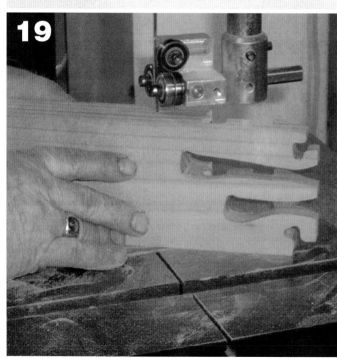

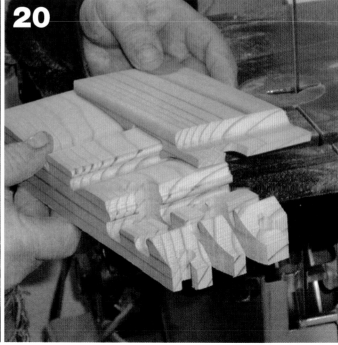

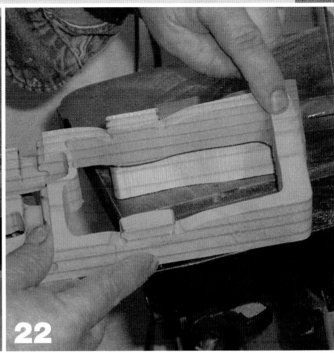

STEPS 21-22 With the top removed, turn the blank right-side-up an, entering through the last cut key, hollow out the body as we have before, but this time leave ½"-thick material at the back of the body.

STEPS 23-24 Lay the inside on its side and cut off the inner lid.

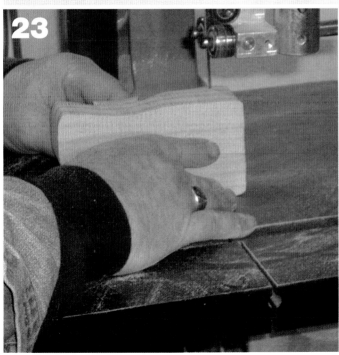

STEPS 25-26   Cut out a corner of the inner guts. Then step the cut in ⅛" and cut again, forming a dividing wall (photo 26, sorry about the shaky camera!) and the block that will be the divider key. In the round-drawer box, the key was cut in the side of the box. In this box, we will cut the key in the rear of the box.

STEPS 27-28   Cut a dovetail pull in the top of the little blank, then cut the lid. Cut two small chambers in the small blank. This is the divider key.

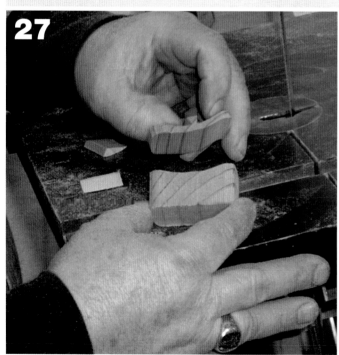

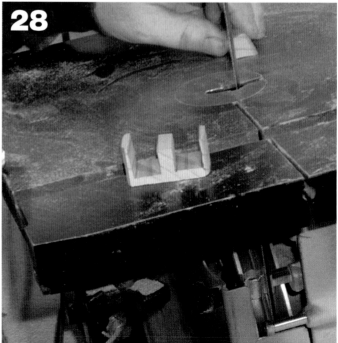

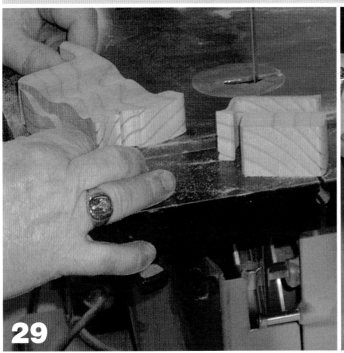

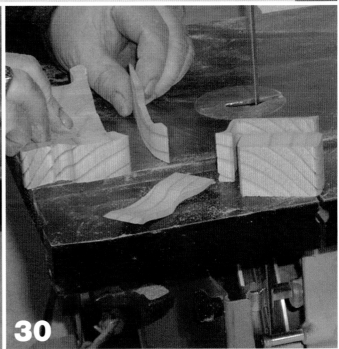

STEPS 29-31 Cut the two shoulders and the joiner (used to secure the entrance cut made in Step 21).

STEP 32 It's time to start on the spring drawer. Scribe a line around the blank, making sure to flare the ends.

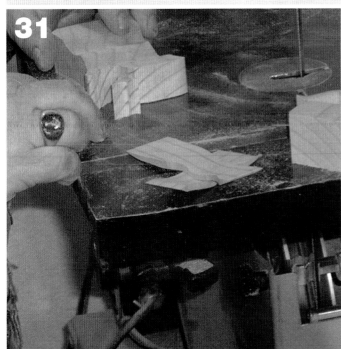

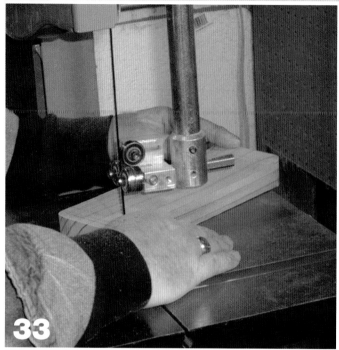

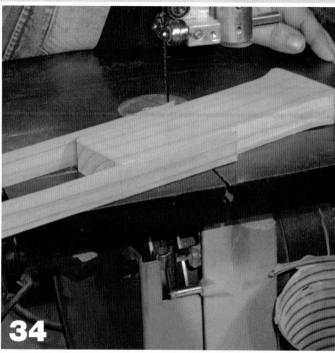

STEPS 33-34 Change to a ⅛" × .020" × 14T blade and cut out the drawer along the scribed lines. This thinner blade cuts away less wood, so the drawer will fit a little better.

STEPS 35-36 Cross cut the spring drawer blank about two-thirds from the front of the blank.

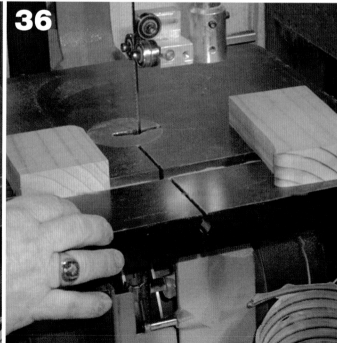

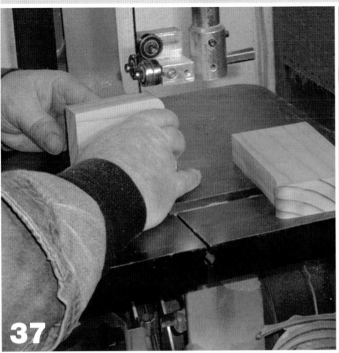

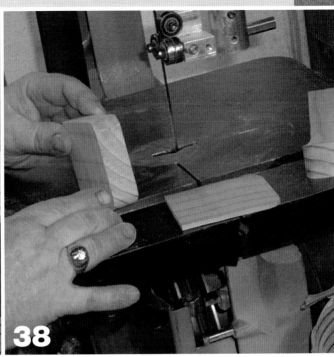

STEPS 37-38 The shorter blank will be the hidden drawer. Cut off the bottom from this blank.

STEPS 39-40 Cut out the middle of the drawer, leaving ¼"-thick sides.

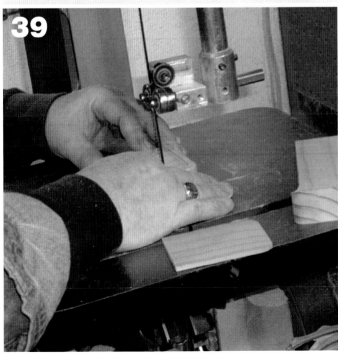

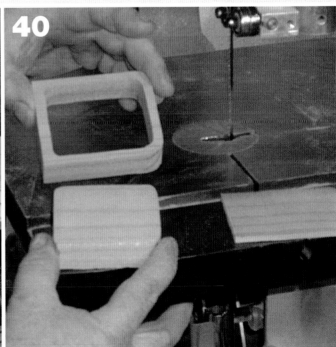

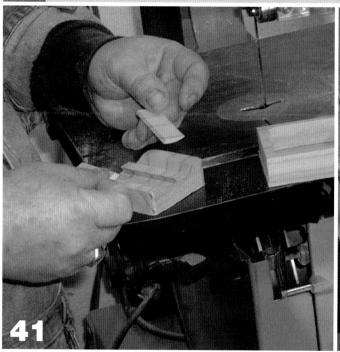

STEPS 41-42   Cut a dovetail-shaped handle in the top of the guts. Then cut the lid from the guts.

STEPS 43-44   Now cut the shoulders from the guts. This drawer is now ready to be glued back together.

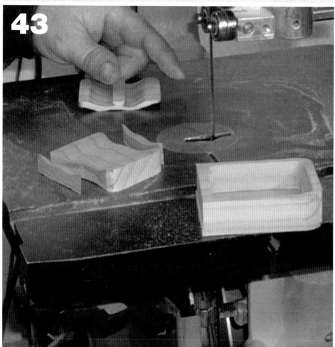

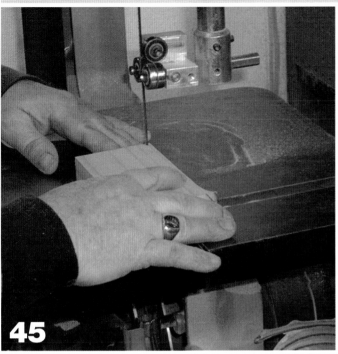

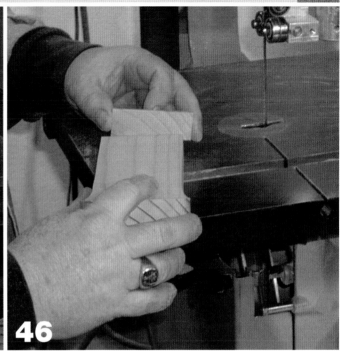

STEPS 45-46   Move back to the larger section of the spring drawer blank and cut about ⅛" from the back of the blank. This space will be taken up by the spring.

STEPS 47-48   Cut the bottom from the spring drawer blank.

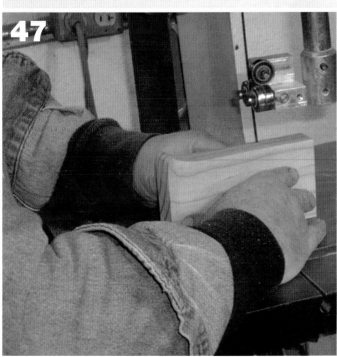

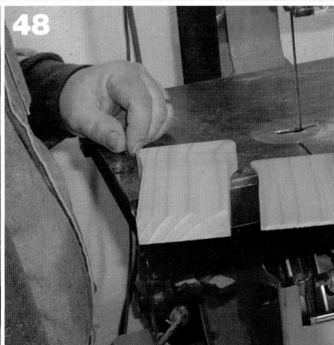

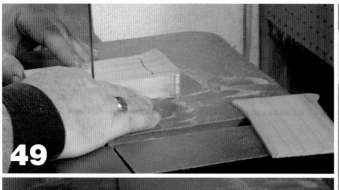

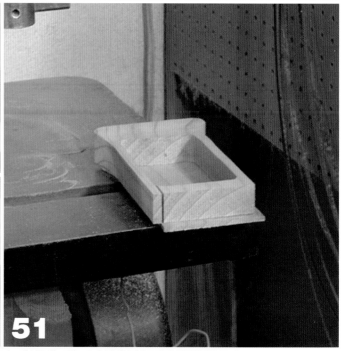

STEPS 49-51 Cut the guts from the spring drawer blank, leaving the front and back of the drawer ½" thick.

STEPS 52-53 Cut a dovetail-shaped pull in the guts of the spring drawer.

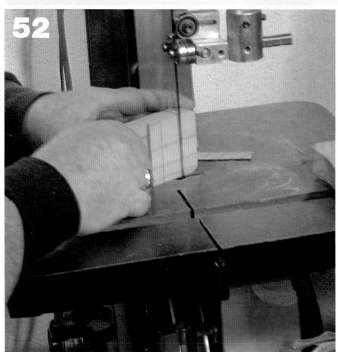

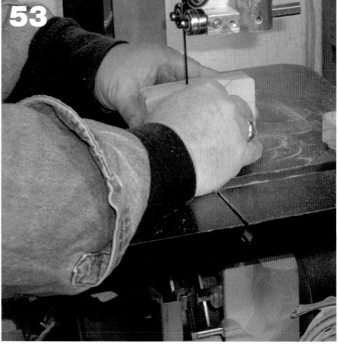

STEPS 54-55 With the pull shaped, cut the lid from the guts.

STEPS 56-57 Next, cut the shoulders from the guts and the front drawer is done. Photo 57 shows all of the parts for the lower level, spring drawer and hidden drawer. The piece I'm holding is the 1/8" slice removed from the front drawer. It won't be used.

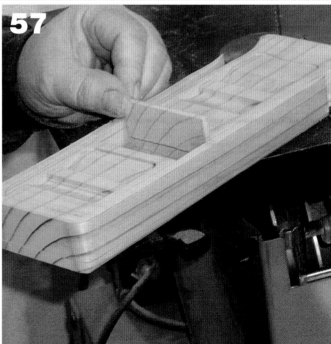

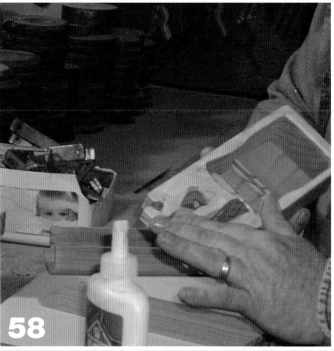

STEPS 58-59   After deburring all of the parts, glue the bottom to the top level.

STEPS 60-61   Glue the bottom to the lower level sides.

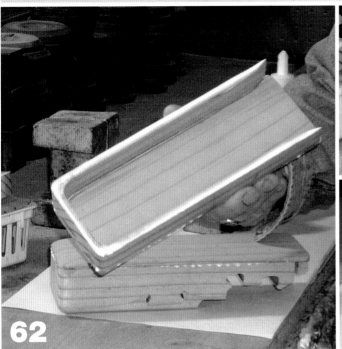

STEPS 62-64   Glue the lower level to the top level, pushing the top level back about ¼" on the lower level.

STEPS 65-66   Glue the entry cut together at the back of the spring drawer. Then spread glue on the drawer's lower edges to attach the bottom.

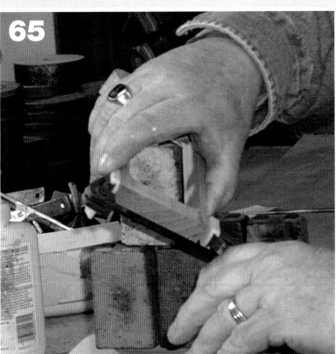

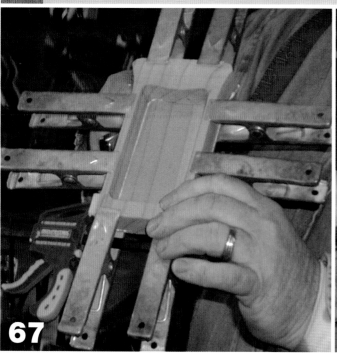

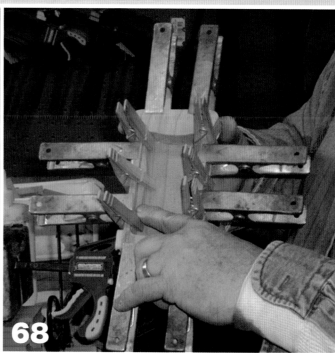

STEPS 67-68 Use plenty of spring clamps to hold the bottom and shoulders in place!

STEPS 69-70 Glue the shoulders for the spring release key and the shoulders for the lid in place in the top of the box.

STEPS 71-72 Sand the box's sides and drawers. Then sand the three tapered sides of the long drawer until it makes a seal in the back of the box. I do this on the round part of my belt sander. When this is done, the drawer will be recessed into the box about ¼" or so. This is why the back of the box was left thicker — so it could be trimmed off later.

STEPS 73-74 Cut a ⅛" dowel that is about 1" long and sand it to a point on one end. Insert the divider key into the framework.

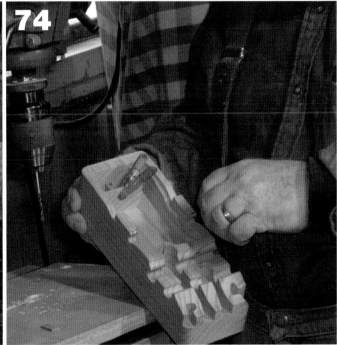

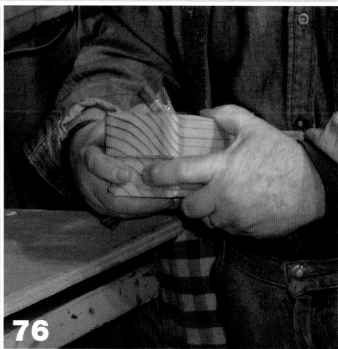

STEPS 75-78   Insert the drawer (without the spring) into the box. Drill a ⅛" hole through the divider while holding the drawer closed as tightly as possible. *Don't drill through the bottom of the drawer!*

STEPS 79   Put glue into the hole in the divider key and on the top of the center finger of the divider. Insert the flat end of the dowel into the hole from the bottom of the divider, add the sliver of wood and clamp it in place. See Round-Drawer Spring Safe, steps 43-52.

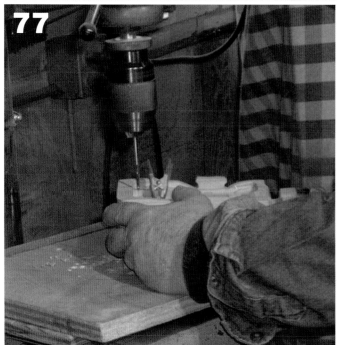

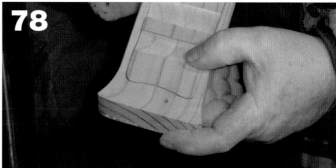

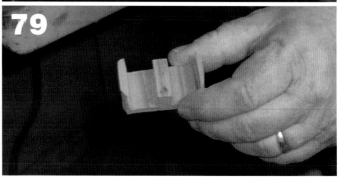

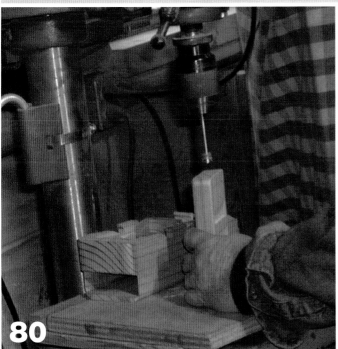

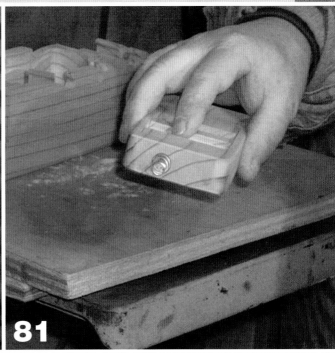

STEPS 80-81 Drill the hole in the back of the long drawer for the spring. Drill it in-line with the hole for the release key. Glue the coil spring into place using a dab of hot glue.

STEPS 82-83 After the glue has dried, put both drawers (with the spring installed) into the box and put the release key in place with the dowel going into the hole. Put the lid on the box and go to the band saw. Trim the back of the box flush with the lower level. Sand the box smooth and finish it.

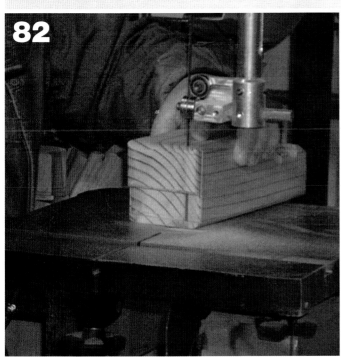

Holes are Cool

Some people see knot holes as bad things and toss
the wood into the scrap pile. I prefer to look at holes as
opportunities to be creative. When you find a piece of
wood that has a loose knot that can be removed, do not
fill it in. The idea is to make the hole part of the box. I've
provided several examples showing ways to incorporate
holes into puzzle box designs in the following photos.

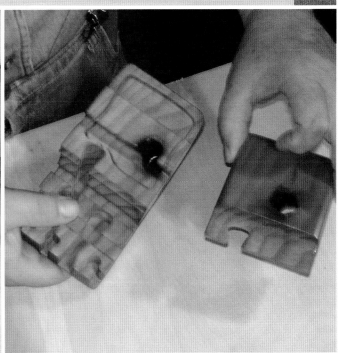

This hole starts in the side and goes through the top.

Cut out the box as you normally would. The top and lid will have holes.

(photo below) After you cut out the guts, cut around the hole and glue it back in place. The hole runs through the box but doesn't interfere with its operation.

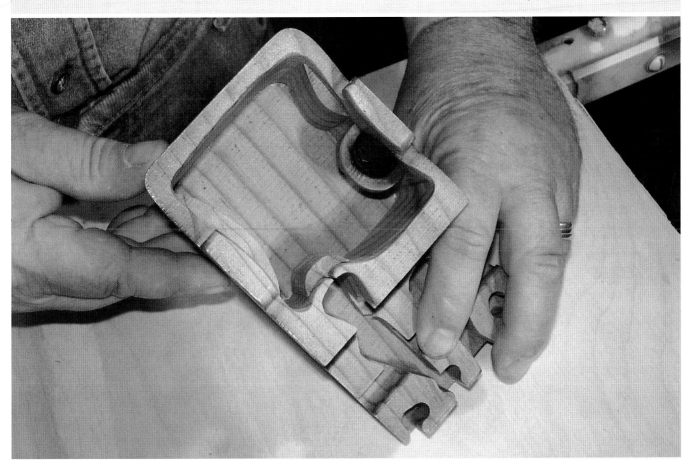

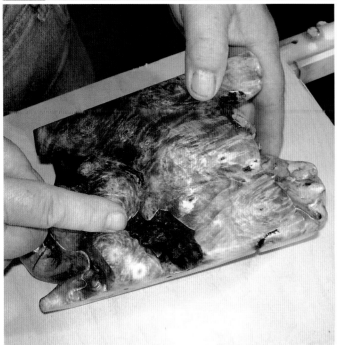 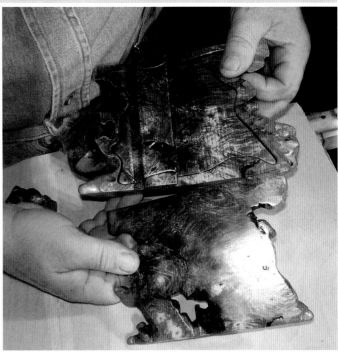

In this chunk of burl wood, there was a hole that ended up in the top of the box.

It runs through the lid and into the box.

(photo below)   But, the hole stops at the bottom and doesn't go completely through it. I left the hole exposed. Neat.

The hole starts in the bottom of this box.

(photo below) It stops about one-third of the way up from the bottom. I cut around the hole and glued it back in place to the bottom.

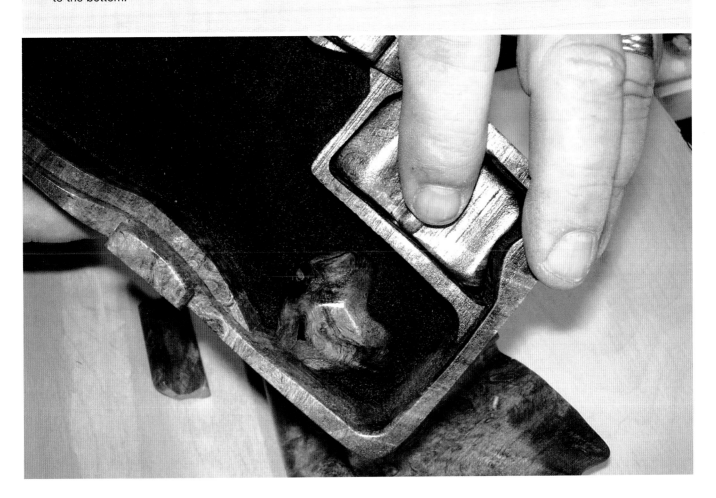

Here's a box with the hole running from the side...

...and through the bottom.

(photo below) Cutting around the hole and gluing it back in place conceals the hole from view inside the box.

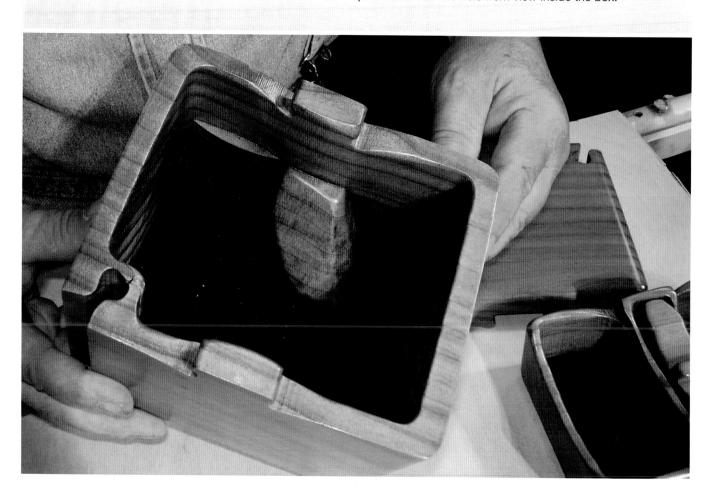

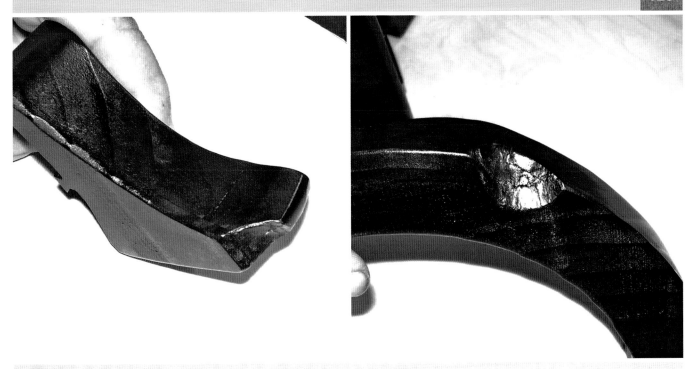

This hole is hidden inside an ultimate jewelry box. It takes out a corner of the center drawer.

And it takes out part of the side and bottom of another drawer.

(photo below) To blend the hole with the inside of the drawer, I chose to cover the inside of the hole with flocking.

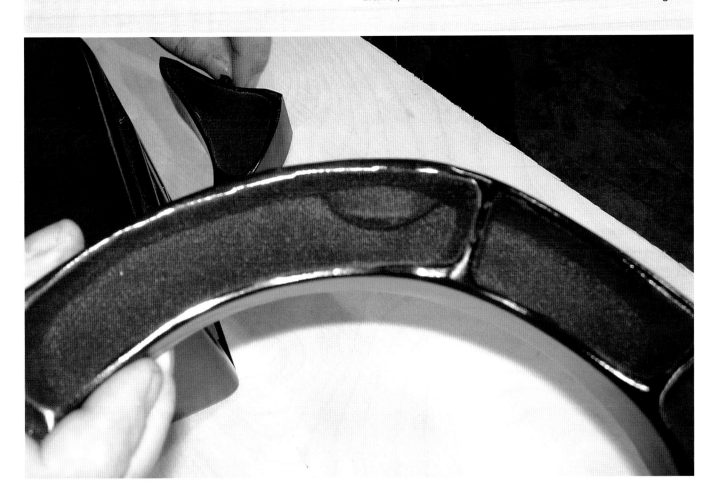

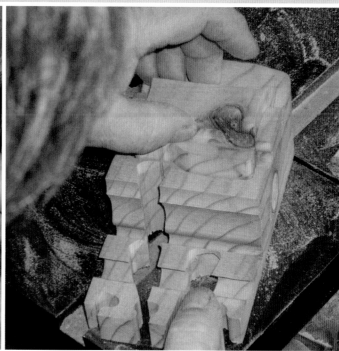

A redwood blank with a knot hole running from the side to the bottom. With this much wood, even if the knot is loose, it can't be removed easily, so don't try.

Using the blank in the photo at left, I've just finished hollowing out the body of a box. The knot is mostly in the guts.

Now I can push out the knot from the side of the box.

A small metal rod will help remove the knot from the guts.

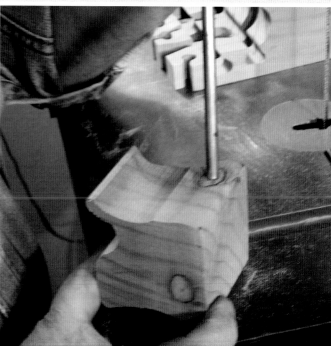

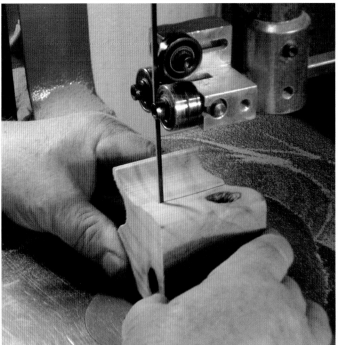

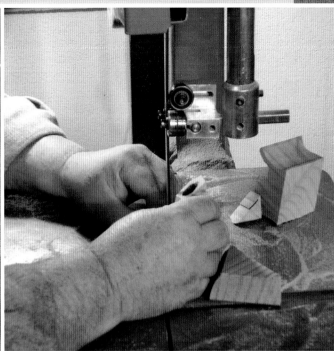

Cut out the hole from the guts. Start by removing most of the extra material.

Now start cutting around the knot hole.

The finished knot hole.

The hole will fit perfectly back in the box.

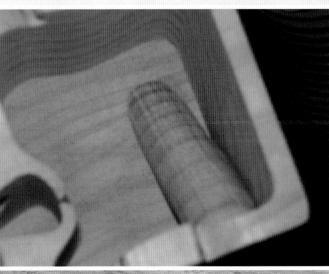

ULTIMATE JEWELRY BOX

The ultimate jewelry box is one of the most complex and time-consuming pieces to make. The first requirement is to have a large piece of completely dry wood. For this box, a piece of wood 13"L × 5"H × 6"D will do just fine. (The piece I'm using was dried in my shop for 3 years.)

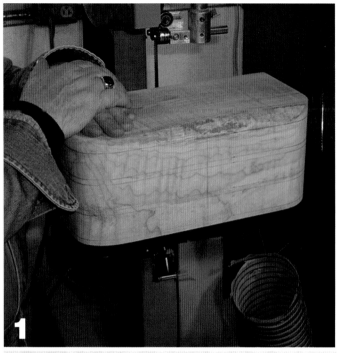

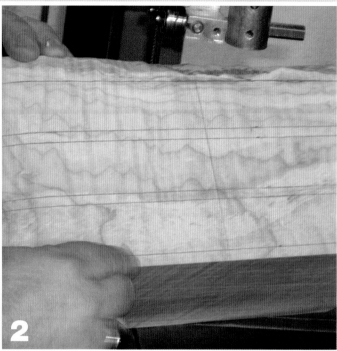

STEPS 1-2 Make sure your blank is perfectly square on all sides. Then round the front corners. This gives the piece a softer, more distinct look. Using a scribe on the front side, lightly scratch the lines for the drawers and the plates that separate them. The piece has three levels of drawers, with each drawer being approximately 1¼" tall with ¼"-thick separating plates. Draw one vertical line in the center of the face to assist with reassembly.

STEPS 3-8 Use a heavier ³⁄₁₆" × .025" × 14T blade to cut all of these horizontal lines.

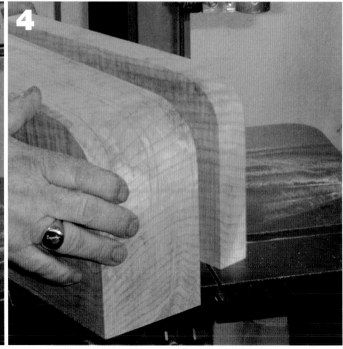

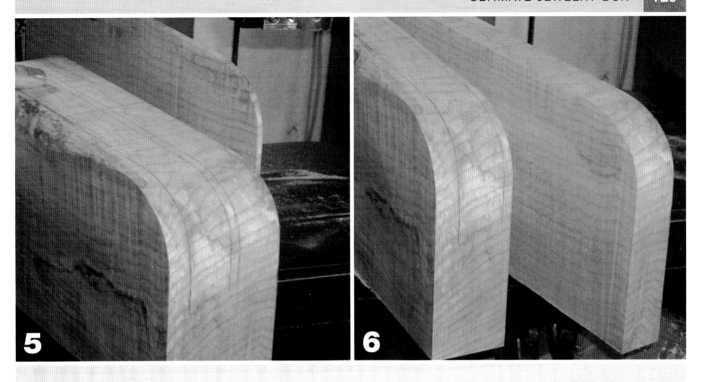

STEPS 5-8 Take your time and cut slowly.

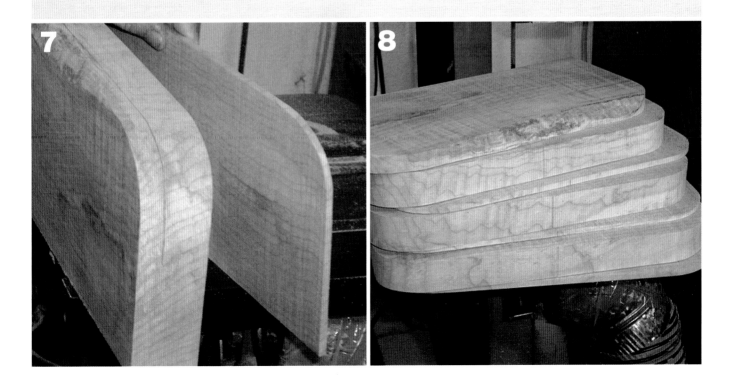

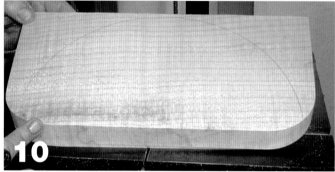

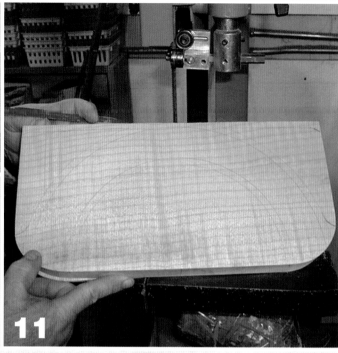

STEPS 9-12 Using a compass, draw the four drawers for the bottom level (two round drawers and two triangular-shaped drawers in the top corners). The center of the compass should be ⅛" in from the front edge of the blank. The dividers between the drawers should be about ¼"-thick.

STEPS 13-17 There are no set rules for the drawer configurations. The drawer plan I use I have found to be efficient, fun and aesthetically pleasing. The second level includes two straight drawers which are designed to hold necklaces. The three other drawers are round. Pushing the round drawers on one side will cause the drawer to exit through another side.

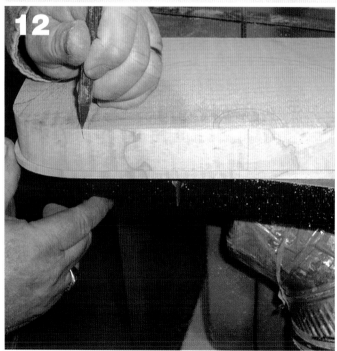

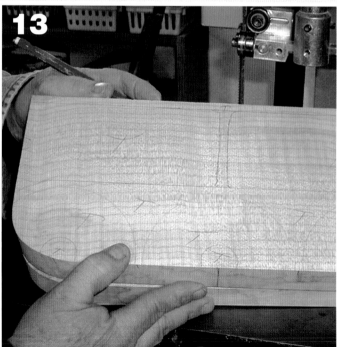

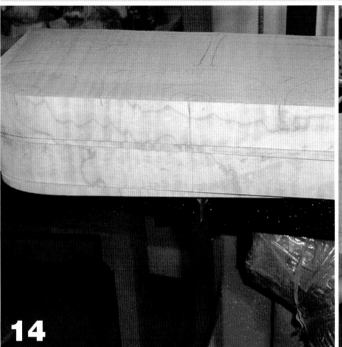

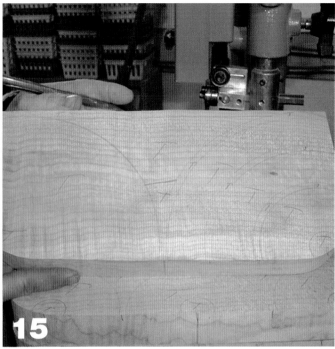

The top layer (photo 15) has four round drawers and a triangular drawer hidden in the back (shown at the top of the blank). As you finish drawing the drawers for one layer, add the top and bottom plates. Use a square as a guide to connect the edges of all the drawers with pencil lines. Do this for all three levels. Also, label each level on its top, drawers and dividers with a small "T". This will help you keep each part oriented correctly.

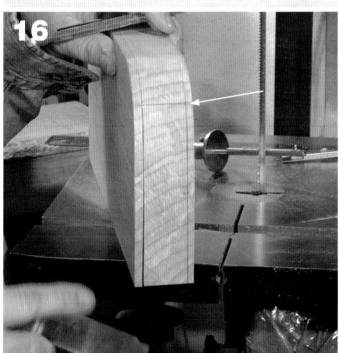

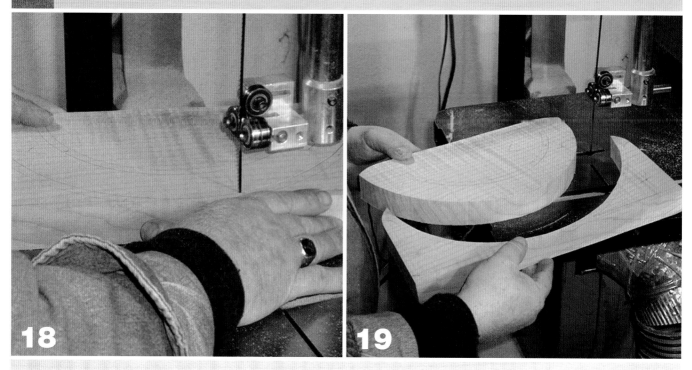

STEPS 18-28 Change the saw blade to the ⅛" × .020" × 14T. This blade will be used for all the internal cuts. Cut out all the drawers first.

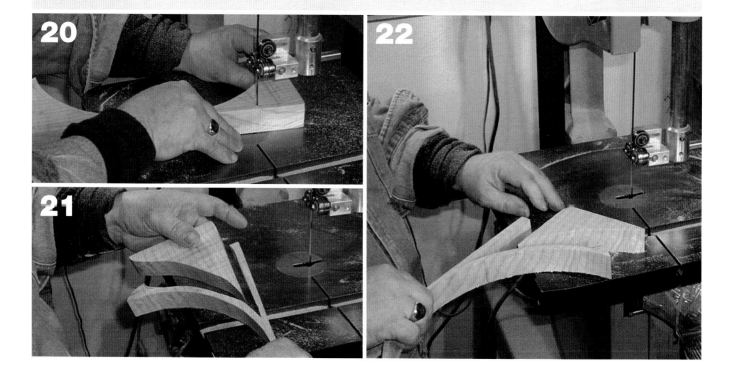

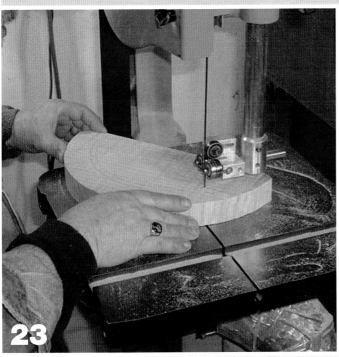

23

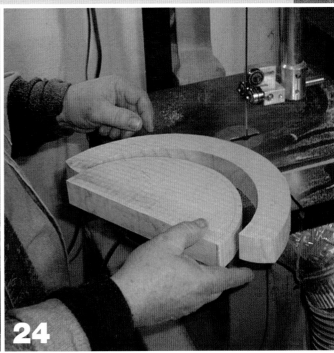

24

As you cut each piece, put it back with the piece it
came from (step 28 next page). Do this for each level.

25

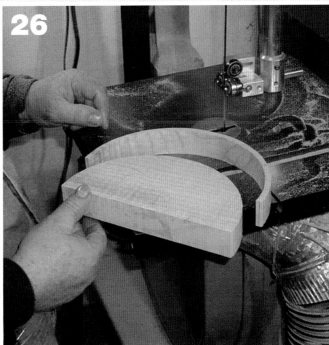

26

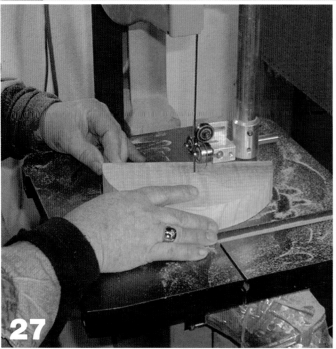

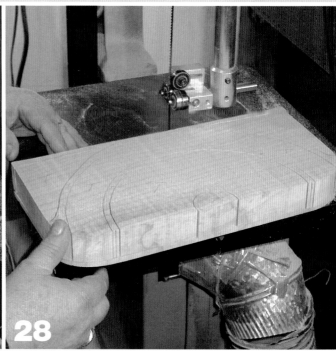

STEPS 18-28 *(continued)*

STEPS 29-30   Cut off the drawer bottoms. These only need to be about ⅛" thick. The easiest and safest way to cut the bottoms off is to put the outside curves of the drawers against the saw table and feed them through the blade, turning the drawer to keep the bottom against the table where the cut is being made. These keeps the downward pressure of the turning saw blade on the table at the throat plate.

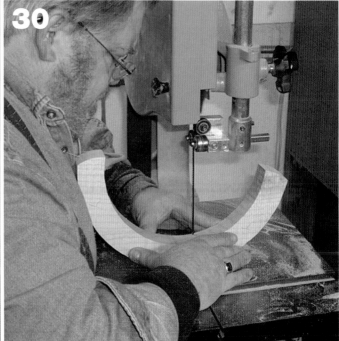

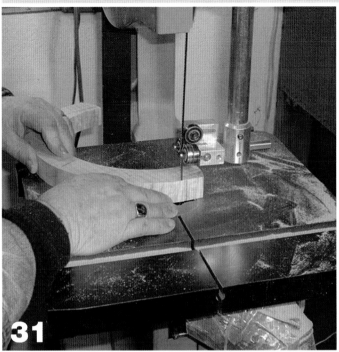

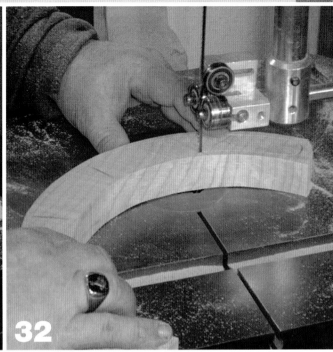

STEPS 31-34 Draw ⅛"-thick walls on each of your drawers to guide your cuts. Then start hollowing out the drawers by making a cut in the side of the drawer blank. Continue cutting on the lines.

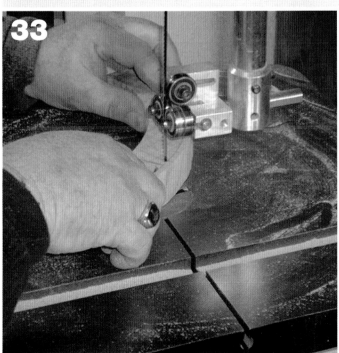

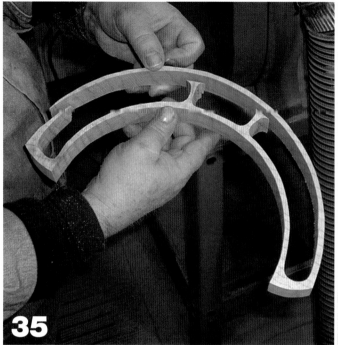

35

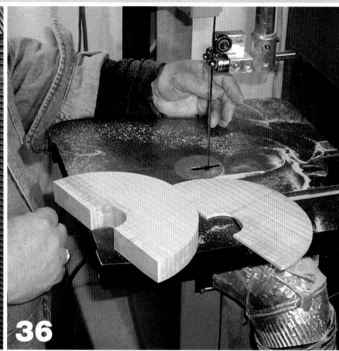

36

STEP 35 When cutting the dividers, flair the ends. This looks good and makes the transition in and out of the corners smooth.

STEPS 36-38 Cut the bottom off the large curved drawer. Then, starting at the side of the drawer, cut out the inside.

STEPS 39-41 On the top level of this box, there is one large drawer on the left side. There are three drawers on the opposite side, coming out the front and right side. What remains is a triangular shaped piece of wood in the middle. This will be a hidden drawer. It will be accessed by removing the large drawer on the left, and, using the longest of the three drawers on the right, magnetically pulling out the hidden drawer. After cutting the bottom from the hidden drawer and the long drawer on the right, drill a ¼" hole in the right, back corner of the long drawer and in the front, left end of the hidden

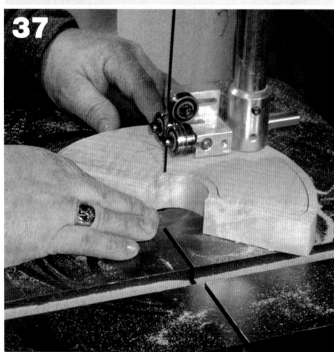

37

38

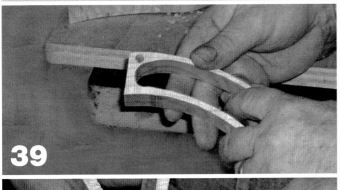

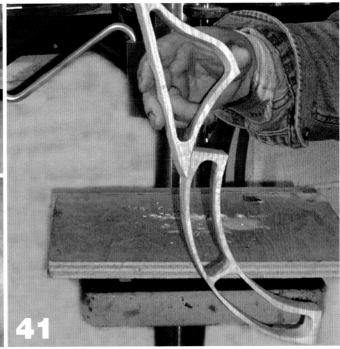

drawer. Magnets will be inserted into these holes. The magnets are ¼" × ½", purchased from www.kj-magnetics.com. The poles are split down the length of the magnets.

STEP 42   Use small spring clamps to hold the drawer seams until the glue dries. Do this for all of the drawers.

STEP 43-51   While the drawers are drying, start gluing up the layers and the drawer dividers. Start with the lower level.

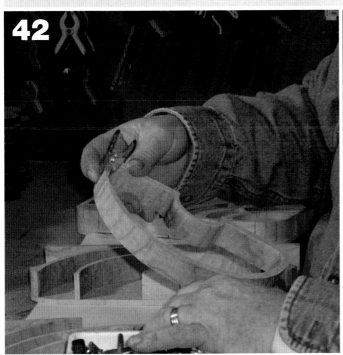

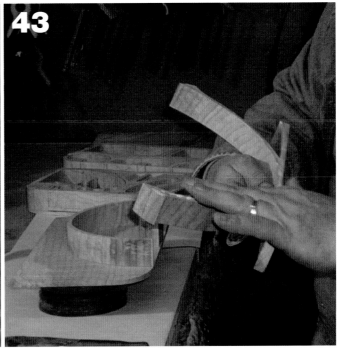

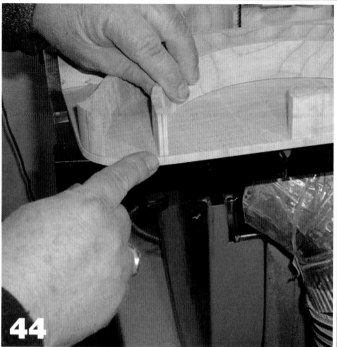

44

45

STEPS 44-51 While the drawers are drying, start gluing up the layers and the drawer dividers. Start with the lower level. Use the pencil lines to help align all the parts properly. Because the glue can act as a lubricant, the parts can (and will!) slide around. Be absolutely certain that they don't. Apply weights and use spring clamps around all

edges. Use glue sparingly on the inside drawer dividers. The drawers will not work properly if glue is allowed to squeeze out from the dividers, and, if glue squeezes out in there, you can't get in to remove it.

As you glue each layer, let the glue dry for about 15 minutes, then unclamp and add the next layer, let the glue dry for 15 minutes, unclamp and so forth.

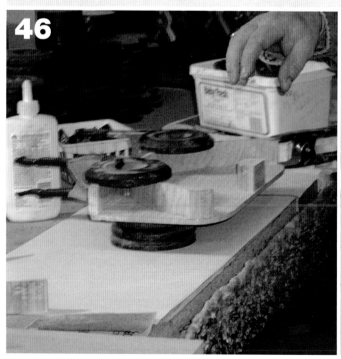

46

47

Author's note: Use spring clamps and weights (rather than pipe clamps or bar clamps). When boxes are glued up, the moisture in the glue is absorbed by the wood, causing the wood to swell slightly. As the glue dries, the wood looses the moisture and shrinks back to its original dimensions. If pipe or bar clamps are used, they would become loose and need to be retightened periodically. The spring clamps and weights will "move" with the wood.

STEPS 52-53 You can never have too many clamps! Let the whole thing dry for 24 hours.

STEPS 54-55 When box and drawers are all glued up, some fitting is required so all the drawer fronts line up with the outside of the box. Some adjustment of the drawers might be needed to ensure they slide in and out smoothly. The stationary belt sander is the easiest and best tool to use. Sand all the drawers so the seams disappear. Then, one drawer at a time, fit them as needed. Use a light touch when using the sander. A little off here or there is all you need. I like to scallop the tops of the drawer (photo 55), using the end of the belt sander. This has nothing to do with functionality. I just think it looks cool!

STEPS 56-59 Now, with all the drawers in the box, lay the box on its back so that the drawers are facing up. You will notice that the drawers are recessed into the body of the box. This is the result of the saw kerf and sanding. Start with the large drawer at the bottom of the box. With one hand holding it as level as possible in the box, use a pencil to draw a line on the body of the box, inside the opening where the drawer front ends. Repeat this for every drawer. Now, sand the body to match the deepest drawer. Once this is done, the drawers that were not so deep will need to be reshaped and sanded on their outer edges (faces) so they match up evenly with the face of the box. Finally, sand a bevel on all inside edges of the drawers, top and bottom. Some finishing and flocking and your box is complete!

SUPPLIERS

**ADAMS & KENNEDY —
THE WOOD SOURCE**
6178 Mitch Owen Rd.
P.O. Box 700
Manotick, ON
Canada K4M 1A6
613-822-6800
www.wood-source.com
Wood supply

B&Q
Portswood House
1 Hampshire Corporate Park
Chandlers Ford
Eastleigh
Hampshire, England SO53 3YX
0845 609 6688
www.diy.com
*Woodworking tools, supplies
and hardware*

BUSY BEE TOOLS
130 Great Gulf Dr.
Concord, ON
Canada L4K 5W1
1-800-461-2879
www.busybeetools.com
*Woodworking tools and
supplies*

**CONSTANTINE'S WOOD CENTER
OF FLORIDA**
1040 E. Oakland Park Blvd.
Fort Lauderdale, FL 33334
800-443-9667
www.constantines.com
*Tools, woods, veneers,
hardware*

**FRANK PAXTON LUMBER
COMPANY**
5701 W. 66th St.
Chicago, IL 60638
800-323-2203
www.paxtonwood.com
Wood, hardware, tools, books

THE HOME DEPOT
2455 Paces Ferry Rd. NW
Atlanta, GA 30339
800-430-3376 (U.S.)
800-628-0525 (Canada)
www.homedepot.com
*Woodworking tools, supplies
and hardware*

KLINGSPOR ABRASIVES INC.
2555 Tate Blvd. SE
Hickory, N.C. 28602
800-645-5555
www.klingspor.com
Sandpaper of all kinds

LEE VALLEY TOOLS LTD.
P.O. Box 1780
Ogdensburg, NY 13669-6780
800-871-8158 (U.S.)
800-267-8767 (Canada)
www.leevalley.com
*Woodworking tools and
hardware*

LOWE'S COMPANIES, INC.
P.O. Box 1111
North Wilkesboro, NC 28656
800-445-6937
www.lowes.com
*Woodworking tools, supplies
and hardware*

MAGCRAFT
National Imports LLC
1934 Old Gallows Road
Suite 350
Vienna, VA 22182
888-774-6005
www.rare-earth-magnets.com
*Rare-earth magnets of every
size and shape*

**ROCKLER WOODWORKING AND
HARDWARE**
4365 Willow Dr.
Medina, MN 55340
800-279-4441
www.rockler.com
*Woodworking tools, hardware,
books, DonJer Suede Tex
(flocking) and supplies*

SAND-RITE MANUFACTURING CO.
321 North Justine St.
Chicago, IL 60607
800-521-2318
www.sand-rite.com
*Brush Head (Flap) and
Pneumatic Drum Sanders*

TOOL TREND LTD.
140 Snow Blvd. Unit 1
Concord, ON
Canada L4K 4C1
416-663-8665
*Woodworking tools and
hardware*

**TREND MACHINERY & CUTTING
TOOLS LTD.**
Odhams Trading Estate
St. Albans Rd.
Watford
Hertfordshire, U.K.
WD24 7TR
01923 224657
www.trendmachinery.co.uk
*Woodworking tools and
hardware*

WATERLOX COATINGS
908 Meech Ave.
Cleveland, OH 44105
800-321-0377
www.waterlox.com
Finishing supplies

WOODCRAFT SUPPLY LLC
1177 Rosemar Rd.
P.O. Box 1686
Parkersburg, WV 26102
800-535-4482
www.woodcraft.com
Woodworking hardware

WOODWORKER'S HARDWARE
P.O. Box 180
Sauk Rapids, MN 56379-0180
800-383-0130
www.wwhardware.com
Woodworking hardware

WOODWORKER'S SUPPLY
1108 N. Glenn Rd.
Casper, WY 82601
800-645-9292
http://woodworker.com
*Woodworking tools and
accessories, finishing supplies,
books and plans*

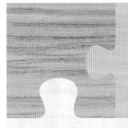

INDEX

A
aromatic cedar 81

B
band saw 4, 8-10, 12
blade 9-13, 17, 22, 32, 44, 54,
    57, 70, 85-86, 88, 106,
    128, 132, 134
belt sander 16, 32, 65, 92,
    115, 140
blank (box) 3-4, 8, 13, 16,
    24-28, 38, 50, 84, 98, 103-
    107, 109-110, 124, 128,
    130-131, 135
Box in a Log 5, 48, 68
burl 3, 13, 120

D
Deft 3, 35, 67
divider key 3, 94, 104, 115-116

F
First Box 4, 8, 24
finish 61, 67, 81, 95, 117
flapper sander 3, 34, 66
flocking 3, 123, 141

G
guts 3, 27-28, 40, 58-61, 74,
    77-78, 84-85, 108, 110-
    111, 119, 124, 125

H
holes 5, 48, 61, 64, 118-119,
    120-125

J
joiner 3, 40-41, 47, 76, 105

K
key 3, 25-28, 30-33, 38-40,
    50, 52-56, 58, 61, 74, 84-
    86, 92, 94, 99, 100-104,
    114-117
knot holes 118

M
magnets 4, 8, 14

P
Projects
    Box in a Log 5, 48, 68
    First Box 4, 8, 24
    Round-Drawer Spring Box
    5, 48, 82
    The King's Safe 5, 48
    The Next Step Up 4, 8, 38
    Two-Drawer Spring Safe 5,
    48, 96
    Ultimate Jewelry Box 5, 48,
    126

R
Round-Drawer Spring Box 5,
    48, 82

S
shoulders 3, 29, 31, 40-41, 47,
    60, 65, 78, 88, 91-92, 105,
    108, 111, 114

T
tear out 3, 32-33
The King's Safe 5, 48
The Next Step Up 4, 8, 38
Two-Drawer Spring Safe 5,
    48, 96

U
Ultimate Jewelry Box 5, 48,
    126

W
Wood 4, 8, 13
    aromatic cedar 81
    burl 3, 13, 120

More great titles from Popular Woodworking and Betterway Home!

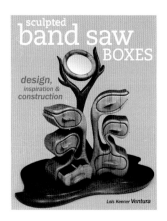

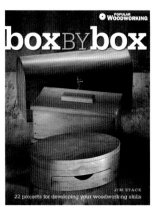

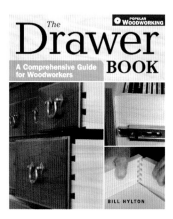

SCULPTED BAND SAW BOXES

By Lois Keener Ventura

Making band saw boxes allows woodworkers creativity not found in other areas of woodworking. In *Sculpted Band Saw Boxes* you'll find step-by-step instructions for 9 new designs, patterns for 20 more, plus a stunning gallery of Ventura's boxes guaranteed to inspire you to stretch your creative muscles and create your own original box designs.

ISBN 13: 978-1-55870-829-7
ISBN 10: 1-55870-829-4
paperback, 128 p., #Z1678

BOX BY BOX

By Jim Stack

Hone your woodworking skills one box at a time. In the pages of this book you'll find plans for 21 delightful boxes along with step-by-step instructions for making them. The projects include basic boxes that a novice can make with just a few hand tools to projects that will provide experienced woodworkers with an exciting challenge.

ISBN 13: 978-1-55870-774-0
ISBN 10: 1-55870-774-3,
hardcover w/ concealed wire-o,
144 p., # 70725

THE DRAWER BOOK

By Bill Hylton

The Drawer Book shows you how to:
- construct all styles of drawers
- make and use every kind of drawer-making joint
- create wooden drawer slides and guides
- fit and finish drawers

A live-action DVD gives you tons of information about manufactured slides and their applications.

ISBN 13: 978-1-55870-842-6
ISBN 10: 1-55870-842-1,
hardcover w/wiro and DVD
160 p., # Z2007

BUILDING TODAY'S GREEN HOME

by Art Smith

Building the right-sized home involves making eco-smart decisions. Learn how to choose the correct location, how to design the right-sized home for your needs, what are the best sustainable materials, what HVAC units are the most effective and how to grade the lot for natural sustainability.

ISBN 13: 978-1-55870-862-4
ISBN 10: 1-55870-862-6,
paperback, 160 p., #Z2843

These and other great woodworking books are available at your local bookstore, woodworking stores or from online suppliers.

www.popularwoodworking.com